LET US HAVE PEACE

THE STORY OF

ULYSSES S. GRANT

LET US HAVE PEACE

The Story of ULYSSES S. GRANT

★★★★

HOWARD N. MEYER

COLLIER BOOKS, New York

COLLIER-MACMILLAN LTD., London

Library of Congress Catalog Card Number: 64-24353

First Collier Books Edition 1966

The Macmillan Company, New York
Collier-Macmillan Canada Ltd., Toronto, Ontario

Printed in the United States of America

To

Sylvette Engel

Contents

Preface

When I was asked to write this book, my impression of Ulysses S. Grant was far from favorable. The school books of my youth led me to associate his name with corruption and cigars, intoxication and failure. I have learned that this picture is no more accurate than that of the blind man who grasped an elephant's tail and thought he was holding a rope.

The uses of history are varied, but perhaps the most important function it serves is to aid in understanding the present as the product of the past. History is the result of human endeavor in more than one sense: men not only live it but they also write it. In this book I have tried to give an honest picture of the man who led the Union armies to victory in the Civil War and then became the President during whose administration we "lost the peace." If this account differs somewhat from those you may have read in history text books, it is possible that the men who wrote them were giving expression to their own prejudices, or accepting too uncritically the product of others' prejudices. To the extent that I have helped the reader to learn a great deal about a man and something about an era that have been dealt with unjustly by many historians, it is my hope that I have helped to meet some of the problems of today and tomorrow.

There can hardly be a time more important than the present for directing attention to the positive aspects of Grant's life and character. As a son, as a husband, and as a father, he was guided throughout his life by a deep sense of morality. It was this quality that enabled Grant to show what his New England abolitionist contemporary, Thomas Wentworth Higginson, called the "moral insight" to see that the Mexican War "was a contest in which his own country was wrong," and to have the courage to say so. This aspect of his character will also explain Grant's understanding of the "difference between a people's war and a mere contest of soldiers," as Colonel Higginson wrote with the special insight that he himself gained as commander of a regiment of ex-slaves fighting for their people's freedom. Grant's role as a military leader never altered his dedication to the principle of total subordination of military to civilian rule in a people's government: "So long as I hold a commission in the army I have no views of my own to carry out."

We are not often told of these aspects of Grant's military career. Nor are we told, in learning of his political failures, of the genuine aspirations for fair play and reconciliation that moved him before and during his Presidency.

"Let us have peace" was his campaign slogan and his epitaph. But he wanted and fought for justice as the only possible foundation for a peace that would endure. One perceptive contemporary observer noted prophetically, ". . . any postponement of justice is a postponement of peace." These words were written by a young Frenchman, Georges Clemenceau, in 1868. He was then a political exile who was reporting American Reconstruction for *Le Temps*—and who, half a century later, was to lead his own country in a war that brought no peace.

Freedom is never wholly attained but always must be pursued. So it is with justice and so, too, with the truth about our history. If you learn from the life of the soldier who was a pacifist, the failure who was a success, the man of action whose last victory was as a man of letters, that there is more, much more to America's heritage than you thought before you started this book, I will have achieved my purpose.

The downgrading of Ulysses S. Grant as a figure in our history may be largely due to those embittered not by the mistakes he made, but by his supreme achievement: the ratification of the Fifteenth Amendment to our Constitution. It was that guaranty of the right of all men to vote, however humble their origin, that he called for in his inaugural message as an instrument of peace. He hailed it when ratification was completed in words that few have remembered from 1877 until 1965:

> A measure which makes at once 4,000,000 people voters who were heretofore declared by the highest tribunal in the land not citizens of the United States nor eligible to become so . . . is indeed a measure of grander importance than any other one act of the kind from the foundations of our free government to the present day.

HOWARD N. MEYER

Rockville Centre, N.Y.
The day they marched, 1965.

1

Crisis in Galena

★★★★

ON A CHILLY Tuesday in April, 1861, posters appeared on the walls and fences of Galena, Illinois, announcing a citizens' meeting at the courthouse. There had been no advance advertising and few needed much urging to come. The townspeople, like many other Americans across the land, were upset; they were tense and angry. Two days before, the clicking telegraph keys had brought the news that all had feared and waited to hear: American guns had fired on the American flag at Fort Sumter. The "fire-eaters" of South Carolina and the Confederacy did not mean to turn back.

What happened in Galena at the meeting that night was not too different from what was happening in many towns and villages from Maine to Nebraska—and over to California. There was nothing strikingly unusual about the town itself. Lying in the northwest corner of Abe Lincoln's state, near the borders of both Iowa and Wisconsin, it was an older city than Chicago. It had been built by miners and explorers, followed as usual by traders and gamblers, when Chicago was only a crossroads in a swamp. By 1861, however, Galena was losing its advantage; its people were learning that a key spot on the upper reaches of the Mississippi was not a guarantee of permanent prosperity as the iron network of railways fanned out over the U.S.A. Its population was 14,000 (three times what it is today) and the Mississippi River boats still came in regularly, furnishing a point of interest and excitement for the children, young and old.

The April 16, 1861, Galena town meeting was to be remembered in later years because of the presence, in the back of the hall, of a quiet man, about forty years old, of no apparent distinction or importance. He had lived in the town for less than a year and had spent a good part of that time traveling. He had an unusual job for one who had been, as not many knew that April night, a West Point graduate and a hero of the war with Mexico of fifteen years before.

His name was Grant and he was clerk and traveling man for his younger brothers' leather goods stone on Main Street.

The courthouse meeting room, on the second floor, was packed. The crowd was buzzing angrily about the news of the lowering of the flag in Charleston harbor. To many it was a signal to raise their own flag: windows, poles, and lapels sported the Union ensign. There were a few, however, led by the mayor, who wanted peace at almost any price. Others murmured, "Treason." Some said that it was just a fuss being made by the Republicans, who had put Lincoln in the White House, to discredit the Democrats, who had campaigned on a platform of compromise with the South. The first major speaker of the evening, Congressman Elihu Washburne, brought cheers as he declared that the issue was one that was above politics.

"Any man," declared the newly elected congressman, "who will stir up party prejudice at a time like this is a traitor to his country."

The speaker who followed Representative Washburne would have attracted the interest and attention of the audience even if he were not well known as one of the best lawyers—and speakers—in town, as well as a leading Democrat. As he strode up to address them, all were hushed by his impressive, blazing dark eyes, set against a pale skin. Just outside the hall someone had plucked the arm of John A. Rawlins and whispered, "It is an abolitionist fight. Don't mix in. Uphold the party." Rawlins had pulled angrily away, saying, "Forget about the party. Traitors have fired on our flag."

Lawyer Rawlins had done some work for the Grant Brothers' store and had come closer to being a friend of the reserved and quiet ex-soldier than anyone else in town. The latter paid special attention as the eloquent speaker reached his climax.

"I have been a Democrat all my life; but this is no longer a question of politics. It is simply country or no country. I have favored every honorable compromise; but the day for compromise is passed. Only one course is left for us."

The inconspicuous leather goods clerk in the rear nodded his head and joined the loud applause. He had never been much for politics, the hobby of many men along the middle border, and had voted but once—that in 1856 and for the Democrat Buchanan against the Republican Frémont. He had done so because he had feared then that the election of a "free soil" man, one pledged against extension of slavery, might lead to the strife and secession which now faced the country. But with the issue joined, he did not flinch.

He had told a friend the day before that he "was educated by the Government, and if my knowledge and experience can be of any service, I think I ought to offer them." There was a more profound feeling stirring within him. This man who had never wanted or expected to be a soldier had avoided taking part in the rising tide of "abolition" sentiment that swept through the North and West in the fifties. The beginning of his own emancipation had occurred a little more than a year before, when, despite the pressing financial difficulties that he faced, he settled a problem of conscience by giving freedom to William Jones, the only slave he had ever owned.

He knew slavery on the plantation at first hand—through his father-in-law and brother-in-law. His Army service had taken him not only into Missouri but through Louisiana, Mississippi, and Texas, and he felt that the prevailing sentiment of the South would have opposed secession if there had been a fair and calm expression of opinion on the subject. He knew that the great bulk of the voters of the South were men who owned no slaves, whose homes were in the hills and poor country, whose interest in the contest was meager. "They too needed emancipation," he declared later.

After the meeting was over, Ulysses Grant said to his brother Orvil while they were walking home together: "I think I ought to go into the service." His brother had expected this. He answered quickly, "You should, you should. You go and I'll stay and mind the store."

Later that night, the ex-soldier talked to his wife about her father. Colonel Dent was a man he liked and yet the time had come, he felt, to be firm and frank. He wrote to tell him of his decision: "No impartial man," he wrote, "can conceal from himself the fact that in all these troubles the Southerners have been the aggressors." He concluded, prophetically, "In all this I can but see the doom of slavery."

Within a few months the middle-aged leather goods dealer was a brigadier general, and ex-lawyer Rawlins was his adjutant; within a few years slavery was dead and Grant the four-star General of the Army of the United States; in March of 1869 Elihu Washburne, of Galena, was sworn in as Secretary of State of the United States and General John A. Rawlins as Secretary of War. The man who had appointed them was Ulysses S. Grant, eighteenth President of the United States.

2

A Name and a Place

★★★★

AS THE NEWS of the American Revolution traveled around the world, it became a signal to many other peoples to fight for their independence. Reports of such uprisings were warmly received in America by those who had won their own country's freedom not long before.

Americans of the early 1820s were aroused by the fight of the Greeks for independence from the Turkish empire. There was a special interest in this effort of Europe's oldest civilization—the land of Ulysses, Achilles, and the other heroes of the Trojan War—to gain freedom.

The sympathy of spirit that swept the American people left its marks on the land. Homes and public buildings were modeled after Greek architecture and many of them stand today. New villages were named Athens, Corinth, Ithaca, and Ypsilanti. The Greek Revival, as it was called, was not confined to the cultured East; the simple and plain folk of the Middle West, the new frontier of that day, also felt the sentiment of the times.

That was why Grandma Simpson put the unusual name of "Ulysses" on a slip of paper as her choice when the Grant and Simpson families met in 1822 to select by lot a name for the new Grant baby. Grandpa's choice of "Hiram" was picked first, and so Jesse and Hannah Grant's first boy was named Hiram Ulysses. Hannah preferred the Greek name. Since boys are generally known by the name their mother calls them, the child was most frequently addressed by his middle name, shortened in earlier years to "Lys" or "Lyssus." Naturally, when he grew a little older, the boys he played with would call him "Useless." As is often the case with nicknames, this was neither fair nor accurate. He was to grow up a very useful boy.

Few boys have had such contrasting parents. His father, Jesse, was energetic, ambitious, outgoing, and talkative. He was just the sort of man who was likely to induce shyness in his son and keep him from being very communicative. Jesse had not had a year's education, but he was driven by an ambition to be known and heard from, and improved his scanty education by reading every newspaper and book he could lay his hands on. When he was not occupied with one or another of the many obligations of running his tannery—a rude country factory for converting raw hides into leather—he was writing letters to the editor of the local newspaper, or composing some awful doggerel which he thought was poetry, or quarreling about politics with one of his neighbors or customers. It was hardly the best way to win popularity, and Jesse was not the most beloved member of the communities in which he lived.

Hannah Simpson Grant was modest and unselfish, a woman of good sense and devoted to her religion. Above all she was known and remembered for her self-restraint and quiet ways. It might have been these attributes of a good listener that attracted her to her chatterbox of a husband. She was a conscientious worker and did not shirk any of the many duties and responsibilities that fell upon a frontier mother.

Life in those days had few comforts and no luxuries. The furniture was rough and there was not much of it; the walls were bare, the windows few and tiny; the cooking was done on an open fireplace with cast-iron pots and a crane.

The region where Ulysses grew up was a land of contrasts and of motion. There were no railroads in 1822. Outside of the cobblestoned streets of the large Eastern port cities, there was hardly a road that was worth much to travel on after a heavy rain. The rivers, however, flowed on, rain or shine, and cut their way through the mountains. Busiest of all in those days was the broad Ohio River, meandering West from Pittsburgh until it met the Mississippi at Cairo, Illinois. The Ohio was the superhighway to the West that was opening up, and at the same time it was the border between the North and South, which were gradually but surely being driven apart by the issue of slavery for some versus freedom for all.

Strung along the banks of the Ohio was a broken line of settlements which served as landings for the steamboats and the flat barges that were making their way west. Not all of the pioneers were Easterners, for many who, as Jesse used to say, "could not or would not" own slaves were among the settlers from below Mason and Dixon's line who made their way up the Shenandoah Valley or through Kentucky to cross the Ohio River. A village might turn out to have more soft Southern drawls than Yankee twangs, even though situated on the north bank of the Ohio.

Before coming to the Ohio River village of Point Pleasant, where Ulysses was born, Jesse had lived in the Western Reserve region of northeast Ohio, where his father, Captain Noah, had settled in 1799—the last stop in a westward trek that began after the Revolutionary soldier's career. Noah had not been able to keep his large family together when Jesse's mother died a few years later, and the children had scattered, finding homes with families in the neighborhood where they worked for their keep and sometimes learned a trade. By one of those improbable coincidences that fate and history supply at times, one of the Ohio homes where Jesse lived and learned something of the tanner's trade was that of Owen Brown, whose oldest son, John, was already, at the age of fifteen, an unusually vigorous opponent not only of slavery but of racial discrimination. Forty years later the sound of "John Brown's Body" was to mean a great deal to Jesse and his son.

By 1822, when Jesse Grant's first son was born, most white Americans of North and South alike had forgotten that the men who had made this nation fifty years before had been opposed to slavery. When Virginia's Thomas Jefferson wrote the Declaration of Independence, he had included an attack on slavery in the first draft. Later on the Continental Congress of 1784 defeated by but a single vote Jefferson's motion to outlaw human bondage in the territory that was to become Alabama, Mississippi, Tennessee, and Kentucky. The framers of the Constitution, in 1789, hoped and believed that the institution that was so opposed to the ideals of liberty and equality they were trying to establish would gradually disappear. Four years later, however, a Yankee on a Georgia plantation invented a machine for separating cotton from its seeds ("ginning" it) that stimulated the previously negligible cotton-raising in the South and made slavery highly profitable. The evil system that Washington and Jefferson had hoped would die out without political conflict between the states prospered instead and spread from the Carolinas across the Gulf States and into Mississippi and even Missouri.

While slavery as an institution was confined to the South, the race prejudice that it engendered was nationwide in pre-Civil War America. Until the 1850s there was not even much antislavery feeling among the great mass of Northern people. The active and outspoken opponents of slavery—the abolitionists—were often unpopular in their own communities. In most Northern cities free Negroes found it hard to get jobs and were rarely accepted as neighbors.

Jesse Grant's oldest son and Owen Brown's son John were to have a great deal to do with the end of slavery. Neither, unfortunately, was able to succeed in what he tried to do to end race prejudice.

3

Riding, Traveling, and Growing Up

★★★★

Before Ulysses was two years old the little family moved from Point Pleasant to Georgetown, twenty-five miles to the east. Jesse had been saving to go into business for himself and selected the new community because of the accessibility of great forests of oak that he needed to supply his tannery. The bark of the oak supplied the tannic acid that gave the process both its secret and its name. The long soak in a solution of ground-up oak bark was the key to the process of turning raw hides into the sturdy, finished leather products that were so essential to life on the farm and the frontier. Saddles, boots, harness, stirrups—it seemed that all land travel would be cut off without the products of the tannery.

Horses and travel attracted young Ulysses, who was at the same time repelled by everything that had to do with tanning. Just as he did not care for his father's disputatious talkativeness, and swung to the other extreme, he was quite unenthusiastic about his father's principal occupation. His distaste for the work of handling the raw and sometimes bloody hides carried over to the rest of the process. He could not be persuaded to help with the soaking, rinsing, or later rubbing of the hides after they had been "cured." Even the somewhat simple job of grinding the slabs and chunks of oak bark in an old-fashioned horse-drawn mill was not to his taste.

Travel, however—the activity that depended so much on the products of the tanner's trade—and anything that had to do with live horses, were quite another matter. Even as an infant Lys was charmed and pleased at an opportunity to ride a circus pony. At the age of three he often played alone in his father's stable, or strayed inquisitively among the strange horses that would stop at the tannery gate. Once a passer-by took fright at seeing the tot swinging from a horse's tail and rushed inside to warn Hannah, who listened quietly and then remarked, "Horses seem to understand Ulysses."

There was a practical side to the developing gift that the boy had for understanding and being understood by horses. At the age of five he would ride the work horses down to the creek for water at noon and at night. By the time he was seven he would harness the horses himself, although he had to stand on a stack of boxes in the manger in order to be able to reach high enough. Before he was eight he was hauling all the wood that was used in the house and in the tannery. By doing these chores he was able to avoid the work in the tannery; soon he was to get around this in another way. In those days, particularly on farm and frontier, everyone worked at an extremely early age and almost inevitably had to do so on his father's farm or in his trade. Lys's knack of handling and commanding horses developed so that by the time he was nine or ten he had become a free-lance teamster, and often, by getting a load to haul or a passenger who wanted to be driven down to a river landing, he was able to get funds with which to hire a substitute to come in and grind the bark. He won a reputation for his skill in taming horses and training them to step in the special gait known as the "pace," even before he was ten years old.

In his preteen and teenage years young Lys came to be engaged in long-distance over-the-road hauling of freight and carriage of passengers. Though he had to go through wild countryside, where highwaymen might turn up, fear of danger did not trouble him. After long journeys, he calmly made himself at home in large towns and even in cities such as Cincinnati, Louisville, and Toledo, putting up alone at hotels and looking about, in an enterprising way, for return freight or passengers to increase the profit of the trip. He justified the confidence of his father who responded—"He'll take care of himself"—to those would-be travelers who questioned the boy's reliability. He was undersized and delicate-looking as a youth, with a handsome sensitive face, wavy reddish-brown hair, and keen gray-blue eyes. He carried himself with a calm self-possession born of self-confidence.

Life for a boy in Georgetown was not all horses and travel. There would be swimming and fishing in summertime and skating and sleighing in winter. Lys, as a skilled horseman, was in great demand when the snow came, and as the driver on sleigh rides for groups of boys and girls gained some of the social acceptance that he might otherwise have lacked on account of his already marked reticence and seeming shyness.

His attitude toward hunting was unusual for a boy on the Midwest frontier. When the outdoor shooting season rolled around, all went out who owned a gun or could borrow one. Ulysses never would. "Half the time they don't kill when they shoot," he would say. "They only wound the animal. Then the poor creature crawls away and starves to death. I can't bear it." He would never use firearms for amusement or kill for the mere sake of killing. So deep was this prejudice that he would not eat meat if the blood hadn't been cooked out and the flesh practically burned to a crisp, and he could never touch fowl and game.

Education then was but a secondary part of a boy's life. The brief three-month school year started in mid-November. It was not provided by the state: only those whose parents contributed to the "subscription" school could have the privilege of attending the one-room schoolhouse where restless young children and husky lads from the backwoods and girls on the verge of marriage were all taught together. The teachers had a hard time in the schoolhouse and also out of it. They would be paid (and not well or even regularly) in cash, in beef, in flour and pork and corn.

Ulysses, by his own account, was not an industrious scholar. He did learn to read and write, and his performance in arithmetic was striking. He could think on his feet and mentally compute the answers to the arithmetic problems, a faculty which was to serve him well. In his deportment he was quite superior, and while not immune to the caning by beech rods that were so overworked, he received less than his quota. He was always, throughout his boyhood and youth, gentle in speech and in manner, quiet and well-behaved, and totally without belligerence. He did not as a youth, or later, ever use profanity as a reaction to frustration and was able to think and act while others might still be cursing their luck.

His skill in arithmetic was not accompanied by that craftiness that enabled one to make the most of a competitive situation. On one notable occasion his father authorized him to buy a desirable colt owned by a farmer named Ralston. His father told him to offer fifty dollars for the animal, to go to fifty-five if necessary, and sixty as his top offer if need be. Thrown off balance by Ralston's direct query, "How much did your father tell you to give for him?" Ulysses blurted out the whole set of instructions. Said Grant later on in life, "It would not require a Connecticut man to guess the price finally agreed upon."

Jesse Grant was stingy, but he recognized by the time Ulysses had become fourteen that he had enough talent to justify the cost of some form of higher learning. As a self-made and conscientiously self-educated man, Jesse had a good deal of respect for formal education, and while he still had hopes that Lys would outgrow his repugnance to the tannery, he sent him for a term to a prep school at Maysville,

Kentucky, where Jesse's older half brother's well-to-do widow could provide free board and lodging.

This was the youngster's first experience with life in a slave state, but Georgetown itself had been so dominated by Southerners that the difference in surroundings was hardly noticeable. In any case, Ulysses did not mind. His father was so aggressive an antislavery man that his son withdrew into a sort of neutrality on the issue. Jesse could not convince him that indifference was in its effect as helpful to the continuance of the system as outright proslavery affiliation.

The months at Maysville disappointed the family's expectations of scholarly advancement. The academy had little more to offer than Lys had already picked up at the subscription school. One new experience was his participation in the activities of a school debating society. Ulysses took the affirmative of such issues as "Resolved: Females wield greater influence in society than males," and "Resolved: It is not just and politic to liberate the slaves now." In both cases his side won the debate.

4

Reluctantly Through West Point

★★★★

In the spring of 1837 the United States suffered one of the earliest of its national business panics, followed by "hard times" and a depression. With the outlook so discouraging, Ulysses was withdrawn from Maysville Academy and was slated to return to a subscription school once more that fall. During the summer Jake Ammen, a neighbor's son, who had graduated from West Point six years before, returned to Georgetown for a brief summer's visit. He announced that he was going to resign from the Army that autumn to become a professor of mathematics at a Kentucky college. He would be, he said, the twenty-third of his graduating class of thirty-two to leave the service. West Point men were in demand as civil engineers and math instructors, and it was not considered a disgrace for an academy graduate to resign from the Army to take a better position. (Not until after the Civil War did the nation's universities begin to reorganize themselves to meet the demand for a growing country's advanced education in technology.)

Jake Ammen's report convinced Jesse Grant that West Point was the place for Ulysses. He began to inquire about the educational attainments and the political connections necessary to win an appointment to the military academy. Within a year he made arrangements to send Lys to John Rankin's school at Ripley, Ohio. Ripley was not far from Georgetown and in the same county, but a different mood on the subject of slavery prevailed among its residents. It was as Puritan and Northern in outlook as Georgetown had been Southern. Reverend Rankin was one of those rare men of the thirties who grasped the full meaning of the phrase "brotherhood of man" and tried to put it into practice. He had fled Kentucky in 1821, after preaching the word of God in accordance with his conscience, and for the next half century he was to aid hundreds of times in efforts to win human freedom and equality for all men. His home was one of the important "stations" on the Underground Railroad, the semisecret route from slavery in the United States to freedom in Canada. The dramatic episode of Eliza crossing the ice, in *Uncle Tom's Cabin*, was based on an actual winter escape across the Ohio River to Reverend Rankin's home.

All this meant nothing to Ulysses Grant then. He devoted himself to his studies to pass the all-important West Point qualifying exam, and used whatever time he could spare at the town's fascinating waterfront. There was nothing he enjoyed as much as talking with shipyard workers, flatboat men, and cabin boys of steamers heading down the Ohio River to the Mississippi, and perhaps on to Memphis, Vicksburg, or even New Orleans. Young Grant learned from them much about his country.

While Lys was at Ripley, Jesse succeeded in his efforts to win his son a West Point nomination. The congressman who made the appointment had forgotten that the boy's first name was Hiram. The official designation was made to read "Ulysses Simpson Grant," the new middle name having been picked up because it was Hannah's family name. Thus, at seventeen, he was renamed.

When Lys heard the news of the appointment he was not at all happy. "A military life had no charms for me," he recalled later, "and I had not the faintest idea of staying in the army." However, he had argued this out with his father and given up when he saw his father's determination.

When the news came, he obediently devoted himself to final preparation for the qualifying exams. He did enjoy the anticipation of the exciting trip to West Point, which was to include visits to Philadelphia and New York, the nation's greatest cities, and transport via steamboat, canalboat, railway, and then steamboat again. Much as he relished the trip for its own sake, he had a dread of reaching his destination.

As usual, gray-coated upperclassmen hung around the bulletin board near the guardroom door of the academy, where the names of the new crop of candidates were posted. Remarks were made as each name was reached, not all of them complimentary or even clever. Bill Sherman sang out, as they came to the G's, "Here's U. S. Grant." "Does that stand for United States?" asked one of his classmates. "Not at all: it's Uncle Sam Grant," proclaimed another. And so Ulysses found that he had picked up a new nickname when he arrived at the Point: for the next four years he was to be known as Sam Grant. His very arrival was a bit of an anticlimax for those who might have imagined "Uncle Sam" would be tall, spare, and bony-faced; they met instead a rather round-faced, cherubic, almost pretty, little fellow, who had just barely passed the minimum admission height requirement of five feet.

The military academy did not turn out to be a bit more interesting or pleasant to attend than the reluctant cadet had expected. He was greeted at once, as a plebe, with that unique form of mental and physical abuse known as hazing or bracing. Called "things" or "beasts" or worse, the members of the incoming class were required to submit to a constant barrage of orders, questions, and reprimands from upperclassmen. This was accompanied at the first summer encampment by the normal discomfort of a soldier's life—endless drilling, cruel marches, incessant maneuvers. From the free democracy of small villages and farms, many of the newcomers came face to face with the grim reality of military despotism.

It was not to be long before they were to become its instruments as well as its victims.

Lys was hardly a suitable candidate for the organization. He was physically an unmilitary figure, his shoulders stooped from the habitual posture of ploughing or driving a team and he walked with the peculiar clomping step of a frontier boy. Mentally and spiritually he was even less suitable material for the role of a spit-and-polish professional soldier. After having been a lad who had never been scolded at home, he found himself in an environment where he was faced with a whole catalog of petty crimes, which he was incessantly committing. He received most of his demerits for such offenses as not brushing his clothes, not having his jacket buttoned, not having his gun clean enough or being late for roll calls. By the time of his graduation he stood number 156 in conduct rating, out of a total of 223 in the entire corps of cadets. It was not that he was willfully disobedient, or a trouble maker. He was just by training, background, and nature untidy and a bit lazy.

He made no mark at all in drill, tactics, or military discipline or theory. As one classmate remarked, "He exhibited but little enthusiasm in anything." In French and the military studies Ulysses recalled later that his standing was so low that "if the class had been turned the other end foremost I should have been at the head." He did excel in mathematics, a subject in which he was really interested, and performed spectacularly at the riding school. He also attained a better than fair rating in engineering; as a side line he showed a talent for drawing and painting unknown before and unused afterwards. The few drawings of which reproductions exist today show a sensitive and perceptive nature, and a fine touch.

The whole routine of hazing, discipline, and drill did not conquer or change very much his sturdy democratic spirit. In a letter to a cousin at home he protested against one form of regimentation that his instincts told him invaded his rights as an American: "We are not only obliged to go to church, but must march by companies. This is not republican."

Self-control was a quality Ulysses always had. One day a classmate turned up, just before class, with an interesting-looking old silver watch, about four inches in diameter. It was passed from hand to hand, and just as class started Ulysses was examining it and quickly slipped it into his inside breast pocket. After class began, he was sent up to the blackboard to recite. The weather was mild and the doors open. Without warning there was a sound filling the room, much like a combination of a Chinese gong and a buzz saw. "Shut that door!" demanded the instructor. The class could hardly restrain their laughter, as they realized—although the officer did not—that the noise was coming from Grant's pocket. Suddenly it stopped. While it had been going on he had stood at the blackboard, looking as innocent as a lamb. In the silence that followed he resumed his recitation in the most matter-of-fact way in the world—"As I was starting to say, if we subtract *E* from *A*, then the equation becomes . . ." Not until years later did the instructor learn the source of that strange noise that morning.

Among his classmates and schoolmates—covering the graduating classes from 1840 to 1843—were many who were to become division, corps, and army commanders, on both sides, during the Civil War. While he was apparently shy, and withdrew from such social life as the academy provided, Ulysses absorbed invaluable information about the personalities, idiosyncrasies, weaknesses, and characters of these men—information he was able to use to advantage later on whenever he learned that one of them commanded an opposing strong point, or found that he had to depend on another for assistance on his flank or for speedy reinforcement.

From Fred Dent, Jr., who roomed with him during their senior year, he was to receive a very special dividend. Ulysses' first regular Army assignment on leaving West Point was at Jefferson Barracks, about ten miles south of St. Louis, Missouri. One of the largest garrisons of our small standing Army was maintained there, since St. Louis in those days was a *far* Western town. Fred's family lived only a few miles from the whitewashed barracks of the camp. Their home was large and the Dents were hospitable to all friends of their sons who might be at the nearby station.

Fred had a sister. There were, as a matter of fact, three sisters, but it was not too long after Ulysses met Julia Dent that there was only one who counted. When the newly commissioned second lieutenant arrived at "White Haven," the Dent place, he was an attractive young man, with a slender, graceful figure, regular features, and clear blue eyes that were always full of light. He had grown six inches in his four years at the Point but continued to have a gentle, doll-like look, which was to lead, not long after, to his nomination for the part of Desdemona in a regimental performance of Shakespeare's *Othello*. Julia, just two years younger than Ulysses, was a girl of grace and warmth, with bright coloring and dark hair—attractive, although kept from being formally pretty by a slight squint.

Fred, who had already been shipped west with his own regiment, had told Julia, the oldest of his three sisters, to watch out for Sam Grant and take care of him. She did. One of the things that helped break the ice was her expertness as a horsewoman. It was not long before they were taking rides together whenever Ulysses could get leave early enough in the day.

Grant said many years later that it was love at first sight —and that he had but one sweetheart in his life. There were to be obstacles to their marriage, such formidable ones as war and slavery; but young lovers do not often surrender to difficulties, large or small.

5

From Mathematics to Mexico

★★★★

BEFORE THE YOUNG lieutenant arrived at the rambling homestead of "Colonel" Frederick Dent, Sr., on that spring day of 1844, he had already been planning his exit from the Army. When he entered West Point, it had been more for a college education than for a career; and when he left, he had no greater interest in Army life than when he began. His determination to leave the service at the earliest possible moment was reinforced, perhaps, when he was assigned to an infantry regiment on graduation instead of the cavalry outfit that he had naturally requested.

Soon after he settled in at Jefferson Barracks, he wrote to the mathematics professor at West Point to request that he be considered for designation as his assistant when the next vacancy opened up. The response he received was encouraging, and Grant set out upon a course of review, study, and preparation, to which he applied himself while he was at the St. Louis location. His idea, as he later admitted, was to serve out his Army enlistment as assistant professor at West Point "and afterwards obtain a permanent position as professor in some respectable college." Perhaps he dreamed of settling down in a little cottage, on a country road, near a college town, with a little wife to greet him each evening at a vine-covered gate. Certainly there have been few graduates of West Point who had less ambition for military glory or more distaste for wars of conquest. When he was graduated from West Point in 1843, however, the forces that were going to shape his life quite differently than he planned were inevitably moving on.

Conflict in and out of Congress between the free states and the slave states had been postponed by the Missouri Compromise of 1820, which resulted for a while in the maintenance of a political balance. Since there was always a division of opinion in the North, which faced a united white South, this balance meant proslavery domination of the national Government. In 1836 there occurred the revolt of Texas from Mexico, which was to reopen the slavery question as a national issue once more.

The leading proslavery spokesmen had watched with growing concern during the twenties and thirties as the effects of immigration from Europe and the strength of a free economy led to a more rapid rate of growth of population and development of the resources of the free states. They knew that slavery had to expand in order to survive. There was not only the strategic importance of matching the growth of political strength of the free states, but an economic necessity as well. The one-crop cotton system was a wasteful and backward method of using the soil. New areas were constantly needed to enable slavery as an institution to survive economically: on the new lands the profits could be made on the crops alone, while the worked-out plantations in Virginia and the southeast would break even or lose on their crops as they prospered on the profits of breeding and selling slaves farther and farther west. Before 1836, however, the Mexican territory, which stretched north far across the Rio Grande, blocked the expansionist plans of the slave owners; while there seemed no limit but the Pacific to the expansion of free territory. However, American settlers secured permission from the Mexican Government to colonize in its Texas province and boldly introduced slavery there even though it was forbidden by the Mexican constitution. The colonists finally set up a government of their own, and in a "little war" with Mexico won their independence in 1836. Texas flew the flag of the Lone Star Republic until 1845.

A campaign of propaganda for the annexation of Texas to the United States came next. This was backed by Southern statesmen and by Northern financial groups, who had bought Texas war bonds that were selling far below par. The Southern motive was more far-reaching; it was hoped to make four or five new states of Texas, and so add twice that many proslavery spokesmen to the United States Senate. The debate continued until by 1844 the question of annexation became one of the chief issues of the Presidential campaign.

James Knox Polk was the candidate of the proslavery and annexationist party, and his opponent was Henry Clay, the eloquent senator from Kentucky. Clay, however, after beginning his campaign as an opponent of annexation, straddled and quibbled in the face of what seemed to be a popular demand for fulfillment of our "manifest destiny," as some orators were calling it. Why, they asked, should there be any objection to admitting Texas as a slave state? Slavery, they argued, was legal in any state that wanted to have it; the people of Texas wanted to join us; and the Mexicans weren't really "white men" anyway, so that their objections did not count. That was the broad outline of the argument and it prevailed. Even after Polk's election, however, there was still a great deal of objection by men of conscience to the treaty of annexation, and a two-thirds vote of ratification could not be mustered in the United States Senate. The large group of lobbyists working for the move did not let this discourage them; they got around it through a Joint Resolution of Congress which needed only a majority in each house. The Constitution did not provide for this method of approving treaties, but they did not let this stop them.

The incorporation of Texas into the United States was thus complete, and if this had been all that the annexationists really wanted, there need not have been a war with Mexico. The Mexican Government opposed the union of Texas with the United States; they did not intend to recognize it, but they did not intend to fight about it either. The annexationists, however, had their eyes on bigger game. For the United States to have a clear road for expansion to the Pacific along the slavery route, it had to have the Mexican territories of California and New Mexico as well.

The first step in the road to war was the sending, in April, 1844, of United States troops to a camp in western Louisiana, near the Texas border, supposedly "to prevent filibustering into Texas." The forces thus grouped there were to remain a year as a so-called Army of Observation. They were, however, as one historian later wrote, really an "Army of Provocation." Their purpose was to provoke the Mexicans, who had made no warlike moves, to take up arms. When the Mexicans would not oblige, the United States troops were moved into Texas a year later, but this still did not have the desired effect. After the troops had been stationed near Corpus Christi for another eight months, they found a way to force the Mexicans to fight. Lying between the Nueces River in Texas, and the Rio Grande, 140 miles to the south, was a strip of land, uninhabited except by jackrabbits and coyotes, and without value then except to lovers of cactus. The Texans claimed the Rio Grande as their border, and the Mexicans the Nueces. The United States troops crossed the Nueces to settle the matter, and began to fortify the Rio Grande without offering, as Grant wrote, "to negotiate for a settlement of the border question . . . apparently in order to force Mexico to initiate war." The effort succeeded. It should be added that when the war was over, and Mexico a conquered nation with which we need not negotiate, according to the standards of the European nations of that period we paid her for the territories we gained a sum far larger than the territory then seemed to be worth to Mexico.

While the military movements that were leading to war

were to end Lieutenant Grant's dream of becoming a math professor, they also led to some constructive results. His visits to Julia Dent had become more frequent and more enjoyable, while he was still at Jefferson Barracks, without his suspecting that he was in love. He was on leave of absence to visit his parents in Ohio when his regiment's orders to move to the Mexican border arrived. He then recognized the nature of his feelings for Julia and headed for the Dent plantation to find that his sentiments were matched by hers. The young couple were engaged in May of 1844. It was not to be until August of 1848 that they were married, after the engagement survived not only the war and occupation of Mexico but also two greater obstacles. The slave-owning Colonel Dent's resistance to the Northern lieutenant with poor prospects created a problem as knotty as Jesse Grant's testy objections to a marital alliance with a slaveholding family.

Moreover, Lys had suffered a chronic cough during his last few months at West Point and a form of malaria which had debilitated him. Field service with the Army of Observation rebuilt his physique, and he once said that his life was saved and his health restored by exercise and exposure enforced by a war he condemned.

6

The Mexican War

GRANT HIMSELF was to become a President dedicated to the continuing peaceful expansion of the United States, and one of his bitterest defeats was over his plan for annexation of Santo Domingo, as the Dominican Republic was then called. Despite this, he never ceased to denounce the annexation of Texas and the war that followed. It was, he wrote, "one of the most unjust wars ever waged by a stronger against a weaker nation. . . . Even if the annexation itself could be justified, the manner in which the subsequent war was forced upon Mexico cannot."

Grant, while not recognizing or identifying his pacifist convictions as such, was in consistent opposition to war, to military display, and to military interference with democratic government. Late in life, when entertained in Berlin by the German Crown Prince at a military review, he told Chancellor Bismarck, "I never went into the Army without regret and never retired without pleasure." He thought there had been no war more wicked than that waged by the United States on Mexico. He perceived the relation between the two wars in which he fought and later said:

> The Southern rebellion was largely the outgrowth of the Mexican war. Nations, like individuals, are punished for their transgressions. We got our punishment in the most sanguinary and expensive war of modern times.

Like many another young soldier at the time, Grant had a struggle with his conscience when the first battle of the

Mexican War drew near. He detested and deplored the prospective hostilities, but had taken an oath on being commissioned to serve eight years unless sooner discharged. Despite what he felt was the wickedness of our Government in declaring war, he did not have the "moral courage," as he himself said, to resign.

His mood was expressed in a letter to a friend early in the war. He wrote: "You want to know what my feelings were on the field of battle. I do not know that I felt any peculiar sensation. War seems much less terrible to persons engaged in it than to those not on the field of battle." He wrote to Julia that he was sorry he had enlisted, because of the nature of the war, but that "bullets have less horror when you are among them than in anticipation." Later he was to write: "Julia, aren't you getting tired of hearing of war, war, war? I am truly tired of it." The more he saw of the people of Mexico, the more certain he was that the war was wrong. He suspected that his commanding officer, General Zachary Taylor, agreed with him and wrote: "I doubt not he looked upon the enemy as the aggrieved party and was not willing to injure them further than his instructions from Washington demanded."

Grant went into the battle of Palo Alto, first engagement of the war, in May of 1846, as a second lieutenant, and entered the City of Mexico, a year and four months later, with the same rank, after having been in all the battles possible for one man. However, he did win the "brevet," or temporary rank of captain, for his gallant conduct. His performance was mentioned favorably on a number of occasions in the dispatches, but his principal assignment prevented rapid promotion.

Early in the war Lieutenant Grant was assigned to duty as quartermaster of the regiment. This was a job that required him to take charge of all of the practical details of military supply and movement—to conduct the wagon train, to pack and move tents and blankets, pots and pans, and issue supplies. One may not win military fame in this way but it is invaluable experience. Only the unsuccessful quartermasters get talked about or reported. It is a function of success that you are forgotten. It was not easy work in Mexico in the summer of 1846. Loose sand and cactus everywhere, Mexican mules and overloaded wagons, could make a nightmare out of each day's movement.

The most difficult part of the job was the supervision of the wagons and the pack trains. He understood horses but this was his first experience with mules: not just Army mules, but the Mexican variety. It was then, he admitted, that he came closest to being tempted to violate his lifelong rule against the use of profanity. He said: "I am not aware of ever having used a profane expletive in my life; but I would have the charity to excuse those who may have done so, if they were in charge of a train of Mexican pack mules at the time!"

The staff position of regimental quartermaster would have been welcome to many as a perfectly legitimate and honorable way of avoiding most of the dangers of combat; Grant, however, protested "against being assigned to a duty which removes me from sharing in the dangers and honors of service with my company at the front" and asked that he be permitted to resume his place in the line. His commander responded that his protest could not be considered, that he was given the quartermaster assignment "because of his observed ability, skill, and persistency in the line of duty" and that he could best serve his country under this assignment.

On every possible occasion, nevertheless, when he could do so without interfering with his assigned duties, Grant sought out and joined the action. At Monterey he mounted a horse to get to the front in time for the battle, and joined the charge, although he was the only mounted man, and thus a special target. Ammunition ran low and there was a call for a volunteer to take a message asking for new supplies from the rear. The streets were swept by a crossfire of bullets and it was no easy task to get back with the dispatch. Grant volunteered, and adjusted himself on his horse, Indian style, with one foot on the cantle and his arms around the horse's neck so that he could drop to the side farthest from the enemy. Horse and rider dashed down the empty street, within the range of fire from every side, leaped a four-foot wall and delivered the message.

Again, during the battle for Chapultepec, he showed energy and enterprise, this time in helping to open the way for an advance along a strategic road. He located a belfry which commanded an important position, and secured a detail of men to help haul a howitzer to its top, enabling him to create confusion among the enemy by dropping shots among them from that position. He showed a nice sense of military diplomacy, too, as an aftermath of this episode, when the commanding general, after expressing his commendation and gratification at the service, ordered that another howitzer be furnished to the enterprising quartermaster, by a captain of artillery, to take up to the belfry. As Grant later confided, "I could not tell the general that there was not room enough in the steeple for another gun, because he probably would have looked upon such a statement as a contradiction from a second lieutenant. I took the captain with me, but did not use the gun."

After the battle of Molino del Rey an officer who was later to become a leading Confederate general reported: "You could not keep Grant out of battle. The duties of quartermaster could not shut him out of his command . . . Grant was everywhere on the field. He was always cool, swift, and unhurried in battle . . . unconscious, apparently, as though it were a hail storm instead of a storm of bullets."

There was one performance that was somewhat less distinguished. During one of the battles a captain in his regiment was detailed for other service, and Grant became for the moment acting company commander. He observed, in the

BETTMANN ARCHIVE

Lieutenant Ulysses S. Grant gallops through the streets of Monterey under a crossfire of bullets to obtain new supplies of ammunition.

line of battle, that the Mexicans were giving way under attack and ordered his company to charge. There seemed to be no resistance and the group quickly captured a wounded Mexican colonel and a few men. Just as our hero was arranging to send back his captives, a private arrived and drily informed Lieutenant Grant that the prisoners he had proudly taken had been captured once before and were placidly waiting to be sent to the rear. Grant always had a dry sense of humor and in referring to the incident said:

> My exploit was equal to that of the soldier who boasted that he had cut off the leg of one of the enemy. When asked why he did not cut off his head he replied: "Someone had done that before." This left no doubt in my mind that the battle of Resaca de la Palma would have been won, just as it was, if I had not been there.

There is no doubt that as a quartermaster he was quite practical and efficient, in circumstances that were not easy. It was no small achievement for a novice, who did not speak the language of the country, to do the business of the regiment: find harness for the animals and replacement clothing for the men, get fodder and grain for the mules, replace mules when needed, secure wood or coal for fuel. In two places he even went so far as to rent bakeries and run them for the benefit of the regiment, making more money for the regimental fund than his pay amounted to during the entire war.

From his experience as quartermaster, with freedom to move about in time of battle, he got practical ideas about feeding and clothing an army which stood him in good stead in the Civil War. There were other valuable lessons to be learned in Mexico. He observed General Winfield Scott cut loose from his base of supplies when on the offensive, to keep the enemy off balance, and while doing so to live off the country. He saw Zachary Taylor, cool and unhurried under fire, commanding troops without fancy uniform and with a commonsense interpretation of Army regulations for purposes of simplicity. He learned how important it was that he keep his head while under fire—and that he could do it. He saw Lee, Longstreet, Buckner, Jackson, Pemberton, and the brothers Albert Sidney and Joseph Johnston—officers against whom he was to be placed in the Civil War—in action and had the capacity to observe and analyze and retain what he had learned about each of them.

The most profound lesson of all he expressed in summing up the reason for American victory. It was that the poor Mexican peon who made up the army really had nothing to fight for. "The better class are very proud," he said, "and tyrannize over the lower and much more numerous class as much as a hard master does over his Negroes." And to Julia he wrote:

> I pity poor Mexico. With a soil and climate scarcely equalled in the world she has more poor and starving subjects who are willing and able to work than any country in the world. The rich keep down the poor with a hardness of heart that is incredible. Walk through the streets of Mexico for one day and you will see hundreds of beggars, but you never see them ask alms of their own people, it is always from the Americans that they expect to receive.

7

Life in a Peacetime Army

★★★★

It was a seasoned young man, with broader shoulders and new strength in his bearing—no longer "pretty as a doll"—who rode up to Julia's home in the summer of 1848. She was not the girl he had left behind, but a thoughtful young woman. She had met many young men during the winters in St. Louis in the intervening years, but was still sure that she loved her fiancé; with her added maturity, she was better qualified to judge.

Julia Dent and Ulysses Grant had waited for more than four years as the Army of Observation became an army of invasion and then of occupation. They were in no mood to delay their marriage any longer to see if he could find a way of making a living outside of the Army. A first lieutenant's salary was not much, but it provided enough to get along.

They had a small but "sweet old-fashioned wedding," as Julia's youngest sister called it. Several of Grant's brother officers were present, including Julia's cousin, James Longstreet, who was later to become Robert E. Lee's right-hand man. The ceremony was marred only by the absence of Jesse and Hannah Grant. They were happy enough about the return of their war hero son to give their blessing, previously withheld, to the union, but refused to come to St. Louis to be the guests of Julia's slaveholding family. However, when the bridegroom brought Julia to Ohio to visit his parents during the honeymoon trip, they were captivated by her warmth and charm. Jesse insisted that Julia should live with them if the Army ever sent Lys off to some remote post.

Relations with Great Britain and Canada were still uncertain enough then to require the Army to maintain a Northern Frontier, and it was there that the Fourth Regiment was to be sent. Ulysses' seniority in the regiment entitled him to be situated with the headquarters company in Detroit, but some internal command politics resulted in an assignment to barren and remote Sackett's Harbor, on the shores of Lake Ontario. By the time Grant's appeal to higher authority was won, the lakes had frozen over, and transport back to Detroit was out of the question until the spring.

However, there is no place too remote or too cold for a young and happily married couple to spend their first winter together. Julia was without slave labor for the first time in her life, but she had been brought up without the prejudice against household chores that women in some slave-holding families had, and managed very well. News of the discovery of gold in California and the trek there of people from every walk of life did not trouble the newlyweds or make them restless. By the time spring came round they were in Detroit, and their happy life together continued, spiced by rounds of visits for Julia, and the diversion of racing and trading horses for Ulysses.

Their social life was a little less active during the winter of 1849–50, for Julia had become pregnant. Life in Detroit on a lieutenant's income was unnecessarily rigorous, they decided, and Julia went to St. Louis to have her baby. The separation was hard for Ulysses and Julia soon returned with little Fred. He was named for the brother of Julia who had brought them together. The lieutenant's devotion to the baby proved him, as he was always to be, a family man by interest and instinct.

Just a year after the baby was born, the little family moved back to bleak Sackett's Harbor again, as the War Department closed down the Detroit barracks. Life was uneventful for a period during which the presence of the baby made the isolation bearable. Then, shortly after Julia announced that another baby was on the way, a heavy blow fell. In the spring of 1852 the entire regiment was ordered to proceed to the Pacific Coast. This had the same effect as a transfer of the father to Southeast Asia would have on a present-day Army family with one baby and another coming. Not only was the Oregon-Washington Territory a primitive frontier region, but in those days before a transcontinental railroad, the available means of transportation were perilous and rough. Since it would be at least a year before she could make the journey, Julia went to Jesse and Hannah's new home at Bethel, Ohio. Ulysses went to Governor's Island at New York, where the regiment was grouping for embarkation.

The decision that Julia and the baby should stay home proved to be very wise. The War Department made a serious blunder in its choice of route by directing, in the middle of the tropical summer, that the regiment proceed by ship to Panama, and then overland to another ship up the West Coast. The Isthmian railroad was incomplete, and the regiment, and such families as were with them, were obliged to complete the trip by dugout canoe and muleback. There was a shortage of mules, due to the higher prices being offered by parties of goldseekers on their way to California. When the party bogged down at an inland point, they were struck by cholera, a dreaded tropical disease.

On Grant, as regimental quartermaster, fell the brunt of the crisis of transport and emergency hospitalization. He met it with energy and ability. One Army wife wrote later: "He was like a ministering angel to us all." A brother officer reported him as one of the coolest men in all the trying emergencies that they were obliged to face. Over a hundred soldiers died during that trip, as well as many Army wives and children. Grant saw, as he had during the Mexican

War, that disease is a greater danger to any army than perils of battle.

When the coast was finally reached, the regiment was to be broken up again. They spent a day in San Francisco, and had a glimpse of the mad gold-rush life of the new town. Grant was sent north to Oregon with his group. Their destination was the Columbia Barracks, Fort Vancouver, near where Portland is now. There was just a tiny trading post, where "mountain men," fur traders who had gone native, and Indians lived in log cabins near the Hudson's Bay Company headquarters. For the troops there was a fort of the genuine Wild West type, complete with stockade, cannon in tower, and barracks and storehouse inside the walls.

Actually the Indians of the region were unusually quiet; the only other responsibility of the post was to entertain and to re-equip the surveying parties that were being sent across the Rockies to map the new country and help locate and develop the trails that were later to become the roads and beds of railways. None were expected for many months until winter was over, and it was a dull and dreary period for Ulysses Grant.

While the other men amused themselves with gambling, roistering and coarse stories, thoughts of his wife and children occupied the mind of this man of pronounced domestic habits and family loyalty. Much of his time he spent out riding alone. The beauty of Mount Hood, towering in the distance, and the giant spruce trees did not distract him. Nor was he able to enjoy the still dignity of the surrounding lakes or the good fishing they provided.

His loneliness was not helped by Julia's neglectful habit of writing him only one letter for every four that he sent. His letters to her would begin: "Another mail has arrived and not one word do I get from you, either directly or indirectly. It makes me restless, Dearest, and much more so because I know that I must wait over two weeks before I can possibly hear." When he did receive a letter from Julia, his eyes would brim up. On one occasion he showed a sergeant a letter he had received that bore the tracing of the infant hand of Ulysses, Jr., the second child that he had never seen—and then he abruptly took it back and folded it and hastily left the room.

When spring arrived he began the first of a series of attempts to earn some money on the side so that he could bring his wife and children west and maintain them in that wilderness where skyrocketing prices were the rule. He and Julia had not anticipated this inflation when they separated. Attempts to supplement income were permitted by the Army and his fellow officers participated. He failed consistently, although it is hard to say in any particular case that the fault was his. The first venture, prompted by news that ice was selling at ridiculously high prices in San Francisco, was to join with a group that invested in cutting and shipping a hundred tons of ice taken from the surface of nearby ponds. The sailing ship that they used was met by headwinds as it entered the Pacific from the mouth of the Columbia River; six weeks later when it arrived in San Francisco, what was left of its cargo was sold at a loss, for a whole fleet of Alaskan ice ships had arrived and forced prices down. An attempt at farming turned out badly too. In this instance Grant worked with his own hands in ploughing, planting, and cultivating a potato crop—only to find when harvest neared that the market had fallen disastrously. The misfortune was compounded when a flood on the Columbia River washed out most of the crop.

In his loneliness and disappointment, as everything seemed to go wrong, Grant slipped back into a habit that was for him particularly unfortunate. It was a period in our history when whisky was produced more cheaply, taxed infinitely less, and everywhere poured more freely than it is now. It was sold by the gallon and by the keg—handed out literally like water during election campaigns and similar public frolics—and many a grocery store had a cask on its counter with a tin cup attached by a chain to the spigot as a standing invitation. Some years before, Sam Grant had learned that he hadn't the immunity to large doses that many of his contemporaries seemed to develop from its use in quantity. In his case a little went a long way, apparently because of constitutional weakness. He had taken a pledge of temperance when he was stationed at Detroit.

His resolution to abstain from drinking was forgotten now, in his loneliness and frustration. The effects of his drinking were, as before, unfortunate. He grew gay or unsteady too easily. While this did not happen too often, it was enough to be noticed by the hostile superior officers at his new post, after his promotion to the rank of captain and his transfer to Humboldt Barracks in the San Francisco region. The stories as to what occurred are conflicting and there is no record of any charge against him. All that was officially reported was his resignation shortly after his official acceptance of a promotion. It has never been confirmed that, as was later rumored, the resignation was requested.

When his star began to rise during the Civil War, jealous competitors and anti-Administration politicians magnified the relatively minor misfortune of those early days. To Ulysses, at the time, it seemed no misfortune at all. He was going to rejoin Julia and his children.

8

Hardscrabble Years

★★★★

THE THIRTY-TWO-year-old ex-Captain Grant who rode up to the Dent's home, White Haven, in the summer of 1854 faced an outlook quite different from that which greeted the young lieutenant who had returned there in honor, if not in glory, from the Mexican War in 1848. But there were compensations. An affectionate Julia rushed out to meet him. The baby he had never seen and the older child he no longer recognized were eager to be friendly. It was not long before the group made up a close-knit family unit. That was what mattered most, for the moment. Financial troubles are not always easy to overcome, but they can be faced with equanimity when a family is united. There might have been lines of worry on Grant's forehead and a tired look around his eyes, but he braced himself cheerfully for the struggle to make a living that he faced without a skill or trade or references from his last job.

There were troubles facing his country too. Since his return from the Mexican War a series of events had taken place that had led even conservative statesmen to say that conflict between the slave states and the free was "irrepressible." Conflict flared up when the California settlers wanted to join the Union as a free state in 1850; the slavery spokesmen in Congress were outraged, for this would take away part of what they had thought were the fruits of the Mexican War. A compromise was worked out in 1850 which really did not settle anything. Part of the price that had to be paid for the admission of free California was a new Fugitive Slave Law. In making it easier for Southern sheriffs and constables to invade Northern states in search of Negroes who had fled to freedom, the new law helped arouse feelings against slavery in a way that distant plantations never could.

By 1854, when Grant rode up to White Haven, the whole compromise of 1850 had fallen apart. Destroyed with it was the compromise of 1820—the Missouri Compromise—when an ambitious Illinois politician, Stephen A. Douglas thought to secure Southern support for his Presidential ambitions by engineering the passage of the Kansas-Nebraska Act. This threw open new territories to slavery, provided the slaveholders colonized them before the free states did. The result was to sharpen and hasten the conflict as Missouri "border ruffians" began to try to make Kansas safe for slavery. This conflict, which raged nearby, was only dimly present in the minds of the Ulysses Grant family. They had a more immediate struggle to face—supporting themselves. Jesse Grant, by now independently wealthy (for a man of the 1850s, before Civil War profiteering produced the idea of a "millionaire"), was bitterly disappointed at his oldest son's "failure" in the Army. He had written, without his son's knowledge, to the Secretary of War to request that the acceptance of the captain's resignation be withdrawn, but that official, a certain Jefferson Davis of Mississippi, ruled that the door was closed. On top of the injury to Jesse's pride, there was insult to his tightly buttoned purse, for the ex-captain was so badly off, after his West Coast losses, that he had been stranded without funds in New York after the circuitous voyage and journey from San Francisco. Jesse sent the necessary money to Lys at New York, but with considerable reluctance and not until after his son had had to borrow fifty dollars from Simon Buckner, a schoolmate on duty in New York—whom he was to meet again.

The choice between his father's house, and his father-in-law's, was made when he rebelled at Jesse's conditions for further assistance. Julia and Ulysses settled at White Haven. To begin with there were sixty acres of the plantation which Colonel Dent had given to Julia as a wedding present. For the time being Grant lacked the capital to stock and equip his wife's land properly as an independent farm. There was also the problem of getting a house put up so that his family need not live under his father-in-law's roof. But he was not afraid to work with his hands, and rolled up his sleeves, pleased at the thought of having seen the last of the Army. The prospect of manual labor, even after fifteen years of Army routine, paperwork, and security, did not hold any terrors for Sam Grant.

The surroundings were pleasant. The Missouri upland was beautiful country, with groves of oak and elm stretching away against the sunlit sky. Here and there were pleasant slopes of cleared fields, and amidst them ran streams of clear, fresh water. The people were markedly Southern, but that was not too different from Georgetown, where he had spent his youth. One thing that was different was that many neighbors, like his father-in-law, were slaveholders. Ulysses, however, still did not identify himself with Jesse's violent convictions on the subject of slavery. As with many of his generation, the belief in human rights came later as the product of his own experience, particularly with the Negro soldier.

He did have an instinct for racial justice, as when he wrote home from Oregon: "It is really my opinion that the whole [Indian] race would be harmless and peaceable if they were not put upon by the whites." In San Francisco he had observed and deplored the conditions of the Chinese laborers and objected to the condition of slavery in which they were brought to the United States. However, at White Haven he tolerated Julia's ownership of household workers her father had given to her. He was later to acquire from Colonel Dent the ownership of a working man. He did not accept, with the gift, Colonel Dent's rabid proslavery opinions or politics. Mrs. Dent, during family arguments, secretly sympathized with her son-in-law's conservative but antisecessionist and free-soil point of view, to which he remained loyal as the waves of controversy rolled higher.

The immediate practical problem was to bring in a few dollars and to clear Julia's land. This was solved by entering the business of cutting firewood and hauling it in to St. Louis for sale. Most of the chopping, sawing, loading, and hauling Grant did for himself. At the same time, he began to cut and square the logs for a home for his family, to be built on Julia's sixty acres. The visits to St. Louis, riding on a farm wagon loaded with firewood for sale or delivery to a regular customer, were not unpleasant. Occasionally he would meet an old Army colleague or classmate from the Point, decked out in uniform and always willing to treat him to a drink—which he would as invariably refuse. One schoolmate who had achieved the rank of brigadier general spotted him one day and called out "Why, Grant, what in blazes are you doing here?" to which the laconic response was, "Well, General, I'm hauling wood!" This was enough to win him a good dinner at the fashionable Planters Hotel.

By the next summer Grant's family was able to live with more privacy. One of Julia's brothers went to seek his fortune in California and lent them his cottage on the Dent property. There was born the third Grant child, Ellen, who as Nellie Grant was to have a famed White House wedding. By the following year their own log house was ready for a "raising"—an affair in which, country style, many of the neighbors joined. Ulysses promptly named the place "Hardscrabble" as an ironic comment on the high-flown names that some of the plantations in the vicinity carried, and as a record of his own hard work in cutting and hewing the logs for the four-room structure.

The Grants did not have an easy or luxurious life at Hardscrabble, but they were happy together and managed to get along. The community began to circulate stories of the ex-captain's own generosity to those even less fortunate. Often, on the way home from St. Louis with the proceeds of the sale of a load of wood (which he continued to cut and haul for ready money, while farming his own acreage), Grant would listen to a sad tale of the loss that one or another family had sustained, and he could never resist making a contribution. He was known, too, for his skill as a mediator and in helping by his quiet yet forceful way to solve family problems of neighbors who might have had a row.

While it was a hard life, with some sunny days, and some gray ones, the family was never hungry or cold. Later, after having served two terms as President, Grant once remarked with some feeling to an old neighbor, "Those were happy years."

Unfortunately, in early 1857, Julia's mother died, and Colonel Dent decided to move to his house in St. Louis and leave Ulysses to manage White Haven. This made it necessary, in turn, for him to rent out Hardscrabble and move his family to the "big house." A few months later the family felt the effects of the second great American financial depression that was to cross Ulysses' life, the Panic of 1857. Besides the loss that that meant, his wheat crop proved disappointing because of a bad winter. Following these troubles, personal disaster struck in 1858 when, after the birth of their fourth child, Jesse Root Grant, Ulysses was stricken with a siege of malaria following little Fred's bout with typhoid fever.

A farm that depends on the labor of one man, who has no capital on which to fall back, becomes an uneconomic burden when the breadwinner is a semi-invalid or convalescent. By the early part of 1859 Grant moved to St. Louis to make another effort at economic independence. He had been obliged to rent his father-in-law's place and to sell Hardscrabble and Julia's sixty acres.

His first venture at making a living in the city was as real estate broker and landlord's agent, in partnership with a relative by marriage. He did not have the personality or temper-

BETTMANN ARCHIVE

"Hardscrabble," the four-room log house Ulysses S. Grant built for his family in 1855.

ament to succeed in an enterprise that required both the wily craft of a canny trader and the hardness of heart of a good rent collector. It was not many months before the partnership of Grant & Boggs was broken up.

He then aspired to the post of County Engineer, for which he was qualified because of his West Point training and experience as a quartermaster. He lost out for the ironic reason that he was regarded as a Democrat and relative of slaveholders; the free-soil group dominated the appointing commission, 3–2. For a brief period he obtained a position in the custom house—and then lost that when the man who had appointed him died, and a new group of office seekers were taken care of by the successor.

These days of deepening adversity were days of increasing trial for his country. "It made my blood run cold," he said, "to hear friends of mine, Southern men, as many of my friends were, deliberately discuss the dissolution of the Union as though it were a tariff bill. I could not endure it." Quietly, and without fanfare, he walked into the courthouse one day and cast his own vote on the issue that was dividing his friends and that was soon to divide his country. He filed a legal paper, referring to the one slave that he had owned, William Jones, declaring, "I do hereby manumit, emancipate and set free said William from slavery forever." Thus, he gave up, at a time when he needed it badly, the thousand dollars or more that he could have secured had he chosen to sell William.

His troubles became unbearable when the man to whom he had sold Hardscrabble defaulted on a promissory note, and the money that he had anticipated from that transaction was clearly going to be delayed months or years. He swallowed his pride and summoned his courage to go to Jesse Grant and ask for help. That was how he came to be, when the crisis of Civil War arrived, a clerk and leather goods salesman in Galena, Illinois, in the Grant Brothers' store where Jesse had set up Ulysses' brothers, Orvil and Simpson.

Defeat had not blunted Ulysses' will to do his duty. Neither had it taken the edge off that sense of humor that every man needs to survive. Shortly after his arrival in Galena he walked quietly into a public room in one of the hotels, where he judged from the conversation that many of those present were lawyers. It was a chilly evening and he still wore the faded blue Army overcoat that he had brought back from the coast and used for six years. One of the group noticed him and asked, "Stranger here?" "Yes," answered Grant. "Traveled far?" the man asked. "Far enough," was the answer. Deciding to wisecrack, the lawyer said, "Looks like you might have been through hell." "I have," said Ulysses. "Well," pressed the lawyer, "how did you find things down there?" "Oh, much the same as in Galena—lawyers nearest the fire."

9

Slavery's War on the Union

★★★★

WHEN THE ex-captain, who had never wanted to be in the Army, and who was now leaving the first job in which he had had any security to rejoin it, wrote to his father-in-law in April, 1861, "In all this I can but see the doom of slavery," he showed a genuine sense of history. In the midst of the great and tragic events that were engulfing his country and confusing some, he saw clearly and sooner than many what the war was about. It has been said the war was only for the Union or about tariffs or about states' rights or about anything but slavery. What Grant saw and understood, having lived in a slave state from 1854 to 1859, and having traveled much in the Midwest and Northwest in 1860, was that the war was slavery's war against the Union, and that even though Lincoln was not elected on a platform calling for the end of slavery, it would be necessary to destroy slavery to save the Union.

The people of the North and West were not prepared to and did not intend to make war on their sister states of the South in order to free the slaves. The active abolitionists—the men who had been calling for the immediate end of slavery—were, as Grant said, "noisy but not numerous." The majority of the people at the North were opposed to slavery as an institution but were not prepared or eager to do anything about it. Many of them believed that white men were in some way superior to men of another color and practiced segregation and did not feel an urgent necessity to end slavery. Most Americans of 1861, despite their racialism, had come to oppose the extension of slavery, and did not want to cooperate with the kind of indignity that they saw in the recapture of fugitive slaves.

But for the slaveholders it was not enough that the rest of the nation should merely refrain from interfering with slavery within each state. They wanted to expand their institution because they believed it had to expand in order to survive. They wanted to eliminate the possibility of future threats by having the Government at Washington suppress opposition to slavery elsewhere, just as they had at home. They felt that they could get what they wanted by threats to secede, and if threats did not work, by actual secession. Grant himself voted for a proslavery Democrat for President in 1856 because there was such widespread talk of secession and rebellion provoked by the possibility of the election of General Frémont, the free-soil Republican candidate of 1856.

Many leaders of proslavery opinion, Southern men, were opposed to secession, but their voices were not heeded. Alexander H. Stephens, who was later to accept the vice-presidency of the Confederate states, said in 1860: "The seceders intended from the beginning to rule or ruin, and when they find that they cannot rule, they will then ruin." There was no doubt in Grant's mind that the people of the South would have opposed secession if, as he said, "there had been a fair and calm expression of opinion, unbiased by threats, and if the ballot of one legal voter had counted for as much as that of any other."

The root of the evil, he saw and said, was that the slaveowners, even though in the minority in the South, governed both the Whig and the Democratic parties. They had come to the point where they practically believed that slaveholding was a divine institution. From this, it followed, according to the prevailing view, that the ownership of slaves conferred some kind of attribute of nobility—a right to govern or exercise political power without regard to the wishes of those who did not hold such property. Their leaders made no secret of their war aims when they attacked the Union. Senator Wigfall of Texas stated at the Confederate convention of February, 1861, that he was fighting for slavery and nothing else. He cried that he did not want to live in a country where a man who blacked his boots or curried his horse was his equal.

The Unionists were fighting against secession. But the secessionists were fighting *for* slavery. And so it became inevitable that the Union forces fought against slavery. Very much later in his life, when he traveled around the world as former President, Grant explained this in a conversation with Germany's Chancellor Bismarck, who preferred, as sponsor of Germany's then growing colonial empire, to refer to the war Grant had fought as one "only to save the Union."

"Not only save the Union, but destroy slavery," said Grant. "I suppose, however, that the Union was the real sentiment, the dominant sentiment," said Bismarck.

"In the beginning, yes," said Grant, "but as soon as slavery fired on the flag it was felt, we all felt, even those who did not object to slaves, that slavery must be destroyed. We felt that it was a stain to the Union that men should be bought and sold like cattle."

A great British military analyst, J. F. C. Fuller, writing many years later, and detached from the partisanship which still enters the writing of American history, summed up the whole controversy of 1860–61 very simply and very well. He said:

> The squabble over the meaning of the Union, the interpretation of the constitution, and the liberty of each state to decide upon its own government, were but the weapons whereby slavery could be maintained or abolished. Slavery was not a secondary issue, as many suppose, but the main issue, which

was confronted by a new world order—the civilization begotten by the industrial revolution.

One of the great difficulties faced by those who fought for the Union, as Grant knew and said, was that the Southerners would not tolerate dissent or disagreement, while prominent men at the North "proclaimed that the Government had no power to coerce the South into submission to the laws of the land; that if the North undertook to raise armies to go South, these armies would have to do so over the dead bodies of these speakers. A portion of the press of the North was constantly proclaiming similar views."

Captain Grant had no doubt and no hesitation. He wrote his father on April 21, 1861: "Whatever may have been my political opinions before, I have but one sentiment now. That is, we have a Government, and laws and a flag, and they must all be sustained. There are but two parties now, traitors and patriots . . ."

Jefferson Davis and his co-conspirators did not look for a serious struggle. They believed their own boast, that one Southerner was equal to five Yankees. When they learned they were wrong, it was too late. In one speech Davis announced that he would be glad to "drink every drop of blood shed south of Mason and Dixon's line." The secessionists thought quite sincerely that the line divided America into heroes and cowards. A long tradition of violence as a part of the way of life in the South, both as a means of repressing slaves and a medium of settling differences between "gentlemen," produced a belief that those who led peaceable lives could not and would not fight.

The error was not on one side alone. "My own opinion is," wrote Ulysses to his father in May of 1861, "that this war will be but of short duration. The Administration has acted most prudently and sagaciously so far as not bringing on a conflict before it had its forces fully marshalled. When they do strike, our thoroughly loyal states will be fully protected and a few decisive victories in some of the southern ports will send the secession army howling, and the leaders in the rebellion will flee the country." Many others in the North were of this opinion.

The North began to learn in July, 1861, that the war would not be over in a hurry. At Bull Run in Virginia a battle was fought which showed that it would be necessary to make preparations for a long, doubtful, and difficult struggle. The nature of the difficulty soon became apparent. The South was from first to last a military camp; the North a democracy and a house divided. The South could "win"—that is, establish its independence—by standing still and defending its borders; the Union had to invade and conquer. The South was so situated that, in military terminology, it could not be "outflanked," for it had no rear to be threatened. A rear had to be created.

An additional and serious handicap that Lincoln and the free states suffered for the first three years of the war was the absence of a qualified commander-in-chief. The most outstanding tendency of the leading Union generals during this period was procrastination and intrigue.

Grant was first and foremost a man of action. "The art of war is simple enough," he would say. "Find out where your enemy is. Get at him as soon as you can. Strike him as hard as you can and as often as you can, and keep moving on." Moreover, he always understood that the time required to improve his own position would strengthen that of the enemy equally. It was to take three tragic years before the nation discovered that he had the qualities needed in a commander of the Army.

10

From ex-Captain to General

★★★★

ELIHU B. WASHBURNE had come west from Maine to Illinois in 1840 and settled down to practice law in Galena. By 1852 he had been elected to Congress as an antislavery Whig. In the following years the Whig Party fell apart and he, like that other Whig congressman from Illinois, Abraham Lincoln, had become a leader of the new Republican Party, founded on a platform of inflexible opposition to the extension of slavery.

Washburne was enough of a statesman to realize in those April days of 1861 that the war being forced on the country by the secessionists could be won only with the support of all loyal Americans of both parties. He was wise enough to understand that within the ranks of the Democratic Party were many who would not tolerate treason and secession, even though they had previously acquiesced in the expansion of slavery and constantly appeased the representatives of the slave states. A good politician, moreover, has an instinct for selecting a man of ability from a crowd by observing a word, a look, a gesture. Though Washburne had not known Ulysses Grant before he saw him at that first meeting (with which we opened our story), he suggested that the ex-captain, about whom he had made inquiries, be made chairman of another meeting, to be held soon after.

As a former professional soldier, and a Democrat, Captain

Grant was the right man to give the gathering a nonpartisan character. The purpose of the rally was to begin recruiting volunteers in answer to President Lincoln's call. When Grant was elected chairman, he opened by quietly stating, "I am in for the war and shall stay until this wicked rebellion is crushed at the cannon's mouth." Then and in the days immediately following, Grant aided Washburne, Rawlins, and others in signing up the needed hundred volunteers from Galena and the surrounding areas in Jo Daviess County. After the men had been brought together, he helped to drill them, and Washburne noted his calm competence and gift for managing men. Grant was busy, too, in guiding Julia as leader of the group of townswomen who were making the needed uniforms.

When he was offered the captaincy of the Galena company, Grant declined. He felt that having attained the rank of captain in the regular Army years before, he was at least qualified to be given the rank of colonel and with it the command of a regiment. He was not a pusher or a self-seeker, and in a confused and hurried country where those looking for self-advancement made the most noise, he was lost sight of for a while. When one old Army friend offered to use his influence among the Illinois politicians, Grant declined with thanks, saying he would not "receive endorsement for permission to fight for my country." Under Washburne's urging, however, he accompanied the Galena company to Springfield, the state capital, for its mustering-in.

In May of 1861 Springfield, like almost every other state capital, seethed and surged with orators and soldiers and contract seekers and glory hunters. The state militia organizations were believed to be the most efficient base for building the national forces; there was no draft, and the regular Army was not organized to permit rapid expansion. Volunteers were pouring in; there was a special session of the legislature, and a turmoil of free advice, maneuvering, and pushing for advancement. The governor's office was the center and head of the state militia, and was overwhelmed by the kind and variety of new problems it faced. At first, they could find nothing for Grant to do.

Within a day or two the governor put Ulysses to work in a subordinate capacity. For the next few weeks, Grant did everything from ruling lines on pieces of blank paper, so that they would look like Army forms, to the mustering-in of the state's volunteer regiments. For a brief period he was commander of the military camp where the new volunteer outfits were quartered before being shipped out. A noticeable improvement in morale and discipline followed.

On one occasion, while waiting for a regiment to be formed in rural southwest Illinois, near the Missouri border, he crossed to his old home town of St. Louis for a visit. There he was just in time to observe the coup that helped save Missouri for the Union. Governor Jackson had been plotting to steal arms for the secessionists and maneuver the state into the Confederate camp. Two loyal Union men, Francis Blair and Nathaniel Lyon—the latter a Mexican War veteran who had hated that proslavery aggression as heartily as Grant—managed to surround Jackson's pro-Rebel militia encampment with their own patriotic home guard, and pulled down the secessionist banner. Shortly afterwards Grant, wearing civilian dress, boarded a horse-car and was addressed by a young Rebel sympathizer. The unique attitude of this type was summed up in the words used by the young stranger:

"Things have come to a damned pretty pass," said he to Grant, "when a free people can't choose their own flag. Where I come from, if a man dares to say a word in favor of the Union, we hang him to a limb of the first tree we come to."

He blanched and retreated to the other end of the car when he heard Grant's reply: "After all, we are not so intolerant in St. Louis as we might be. I have not seen a single Rebel hung yet, nor heard of one. There are plenty of them who ought to be, however."

When the work at Springfield petered out, with the enlistment of the state's first quota of volunteers, Grant returned to Galena and wrote to the War Department at Washington to offer his services. He received no reply. He went to Covington, Kentucky, to visit his parents and to attempt to see General McClellan, who was in charge in nearby Cincinnati, but was turned away at the receptionist's desk. His reaction to these rebuffs he expressed on his return to Illinois in a letter: "During the six days I have been at home, I have felt all the time as if a duty was being neglected that was paramount to any other duty I ever owed."

The log jam that was keeping him from service finally broke when the officers of the Twenty-first Illinois Volunteer Regiment came to the governor to complain that their men were on the verge of mutiny. The colonel that they had elected had no capacity for command and the normal difficulties in obtaining discipline over the rough and ready young Westerners were multiplied. One of the junior officers spoke of Grant, who had mustered in the men only a few weeks before. The governor sent for him and said, "These men are a little unruly. Do you think you can manage them?" "I think I can," said Grant.

He did.

He was to display to the eight hundred men of the Twenty-first Illinois—as to the eighty thousand strangers in the Army of the Potomac that he was summoned to command in 1864—the serene capacity to induce obedience that he had shown as a boy with horses and wild ponies. Without bluff or bluster, or any spectacular tricks, he was gifted with a sense of firmness and at the same time fairness, which quickly brought about respect for both his rank and his wishes. In the case of that first regiment he was to command, this instinct showed itself at the very first encounter. When he arrived, he was accompanied by two Democratic congressmen, who each harangued the men with a burst of patriotic oratory. The men responded, as men are likely to, not so much with a patriotic as a lively and unrestrained tumult. Congressman McClernand then presented the new colonel, and there were expectant cries as at a political meeting. Grant!" "Colonel Grant!" "Let's hear from the Colonel!" they shouted. The response from Grant was a four-word speech that had the necessary effect:

"Go to your quarters!"

There followed a month of drill and discipline that made soldiers of the men. Six weeks of marching and countermarching in Missouri (there was no really organized war as yet) finished the work that he had to do. He was able to report in a letter to his father: "I took the outfit in a very disorganized, demoralized and insubordinate condition and have worked it up to a reputation equal to the best, and I believe with the good-will of all the officers and all the men."

While in Missouri, Grant had his first experience as a commander responsible for the safety of his men and the fate of his mission, with the emotion produced by impending battle. He felt, he said, a trepidation that he would not have had were he second in command. He had been ordered to move against a Confederate Colonel Harris encamped in that vicinity, and as the United States troops approached the top of the hill where it was expected that the Rebels would be met or their camp seen, "my heart kept getting higher and higher until it felt to me as though it was in my throat." It seemed to him that he would have given anything to be back in Illinois. However, when they reached the point where the valley below was in full view and halted, they found the signs of a recent encampment—but the troops were gone. "It occurred to me at once that Harris had been as much afraid of me as I had been of him. This was a view of the question I had never taken before; but it was one I never forgot afterwards. From that event to the close of the war I never experienced trepidation upon confronting an enemy, though I always felt more or less anxiety. I never forgot that he had as much reason to fear my forces as I had his. The lesson was valuable."

Shortly afterwards Grant was startled to learn of his desig-

BETTMANN ARCHIVE

General Grant bids goodbye to his wife and daughter as he leaves Galena at the outset of the war.

nation as brigadier general—a promotion that paved the way for the most spectacular success story in military history, and for the final defeat of the rebellion. The man responsible was Elihu Washburne. The new Union army had been growing, and since the number of generalships was fixed by law, Congress authorized an increase and there were vacancies for new generals. President Lincoln decided to distribute the appointments by states, not primarily as a matter of patronage, but because that was how the army had been built up in those first months. Through Washburne's efforts, Grant's name led the list of those recommended by the Illinois congressional delegation. From now on it was to be General Grant. The new general wrote his congressman: "I think I see your hand in it and admit that I had no personal claims for your kind office in the matter. I can assure you, however, my whole heart is in the cause which we are fighting for, and I pledge myself that, if equal to the task before me, you shall never have cause to regret the part you have taken."

The new general was soon to demonstrate another aspect of his quality as commander—an ability to influence sentiment among his troops so that it would favor the necessary discipline. The Union forces not having reached, as yet, the thoroughly hostile country of the Deep South, it was considered desirable that the rights of private citizens be respected. The wild young men, however, fresh from civilian life, needed lessons in self-restraint. One lieutenant, with an advance guard, called at a farmhouse, pretended to be General Grant, and secured the freedom of the kitchen. Everything was cleaned out except one pie. Grant heard the story later, when he passed, and told the farmer to take very good care of that pie, until further notice.

That evening the brigade encamped, and, surprisingly, orders were given for a dress parade—a rare occurrence for troops on the march. After the usual ceremonies, the rumors of the men as to the occasion for the special orders were stilled when the adjutant stepped forward to announce:

> Lieutenant Wickfield of the Indiana Cavalry, having on this day eaten everything in Mrs. Selvidge's house, at the crossing of the Trenton and Pocohantas and Black River and Cape Girardeau Roads, except one pumpkin pie, Lieutenant Wickfield is hereby ordered to return with an escort of one hundred cavalry, and eat that pie also.
>
> U. S. GRANT,
> Brigadier General Commanding

11

Opening the Road to the South

★★★★

CAIRO, ILLINOIS, was a small, low-lying town, built along the Mississippi River, unsightly, disloyal, foul-smelling, insect-laden, and disease-ridden. To U. S. Grant, however, when he arrived to settle down to his first real command as brigadier general (one of half a hundred that had such rank), it was heaven on earth—the one place in the world, more than any other, where he wanted to be at that particular time. Cairo meant the opportunity to move, to fight, to win. For Grant, the pacifist, it was always understood that the sooner and harder he could fight, the less prolonged the war would be, and the fewer who would suffer.

Anyone could look at a map and see how Cairo, at the apex of the wedge that southern Illinois makes between doubtful Kentucky and almost as doubtful Missouri, was a place of strategic importance. It was at the junction of the two most important rivers in America. The broad Ohio, pathway from Pittsburgh to the West, met the muddy Mississippi, which flowed from Galena and even further north, down through the heart of the western Confederacy to the sea. Cairo was not far from the part of the Ohio where the Tennessee and Cumberland rivers joined it, after having meandered through much of the middle third of the Southern states.

Ulysses Grant did not "discover" the military value of

Cairo. That was evident on the map for any military theorist to see. But, more than most men, he could understand and feel its full potential. As a boy in southern Ohio he had traveled often to the boat landings on the upper river with passengers. He had talked with steamboat men and roustabouts and envied cabin boys who had run away from home to travel on the river. As a young man he had seen his father's business expand along the Ohio and followed his brother's move through Cairo and up the river to Galena. On his return from the Army, during his St. Louis days, the network of rivers and their relationship impressed itself on him again. His life as a civilian had made more meaningful to him than any blackboard lecturer could the significance of the Midwest river network. To many who had migrated to the Midwest and Northwest in the hope of building a better life for their families, there was a significance to secession that was more important than any abstract idea of "Union"; some regiments bore it on their banners: "The Rebels have closed the Mississippi; we must cut our way to the Gulf with our swords."

Even before Grant was ordered to Cairo, he had begun to study and to mark detailed maps that showed the course of the Mississippi as it ran south from there between Kentucky and Missouri on its way to Tennessee. At the same time, he looked up the Ohio River toward Paducah, Kentucky, where, a few miles apart, the Tennessee and the Cumberland rivers flowed in from the south. The Tennessee River dropped straight across the state, nicked a corner of Mississippi, then flowed across Alabama and back to Tennessee near Chattanooga. The Cumberland originates in the east near the Cumberland Gap, crosses Tennessee through Nashville, and meets the Ohio near the mouth of the Tennessee. Possession of Chattanooga would mean the key to Atlanta and the sea. Roads were no better then than they had been in his boyhood; the developing network of railways was important, but rivers could not be blown up or sabotaged.

The Confederates themselves soon realized this and built impressive fortifications on both the Tennessee and Cumberland rivers, just before the point where each crossed the Kentucky border.

Within a day after Grant's arrival at Cairo to take command of that region and the forces situated there, an emergency arose. The Rebel general commanding western Tennessee, in a move toward attempting to control western Kentucky, seized Columbus on the east bank of the Mississippi, barely twenty miles south of Cairo. Indications were that Confederate forces would then be sent across the northwest corner of Kentucky to Paducah, thereby blocking the Ohio River, locking the entrance to the Tennessee and Cumberland rivers and threatening the safety of Cairo itself.

Grant moved fast. Being still a subordinate general, he could only move with permission, but he found a way to get it. He wired his chief that he would start for Paducah at once unless forbidden. Receiving no reply, he embarked two regiments on river steamers at the Cairo wharves and sped up the Ohio River to seize the key Kentucky river city without firing a shot. This prompt and decisive action not only helped to keep the Union foot in the doorway to the South; it reinforced the determination of the Kentucky legislature to remain loyal to the Union and helped them ultimately to overcome the plans of their secession-minded governor. It has been justly said that Grant's dash for Paducah was one of the major decisions of the war.

With one important exception, the next five months were a period of organization, preparation, training, and growth. Entitled and required to have a staff, as a general commanding both troops and a district, Grant sent for John Rawlins, the Galena lawyer who had made the most impassioned speech at that early April meeting. Rawlins was but a country lawyer who had no military training whatever when he entered the army, and he never made any pretension to technical education as a soldier. However, it was not with respect to technical matters that Grant needed help, and it was not as a military adviser that Rawlins was to contribute to Grant's career. He was a man of great fidelity, and sound judgment. He became Grant's chief of staff and was to remain in that post for the duration of the war and the troubled years of peace that followed. As his own high compliment Grant was to say: "He was an able man, possessed of great firmness, and could say 'no' so emphatically to a request which he thought should not be granted that the person he was addressing would understand at once that there was no use of pressing the matter."

In addition to equipping and training the troops, solving their problems of supply, and stopping trading with the enemy, Grant and his staff had to concentrate on building a fleet that could win control of the western rivers. Obviously the fulfillment of Grant's strategic ideas required the use of transports, and the conversion of the idle queens of the river, tied up at Cairo and above, was the answer. In addition, warships were needed, and until a type designed for the problems of river warfare could be built, it was essential to improvise. River steamboats were cut down, protected with thick wooden planks, and equipped with naval guns. The officers and men were supposed to be supplied by the Navy, but Grant as their commander found it necessary to provide some of the complement out of his own forces. In the fall of 1861 the Navy appointed Andrew H. Foote as flag officer—a rank similar to that of commodore—to serve under Grant as commander of the three converted Ohio River steamboats and four armored Mississippi paddle-wheelers that made up the midland United States fleet.

Serious problems were presented by suppliers of shoddy material and those who shortchanged the quartermaster's office in other ways. One disgruntled officer, on whom Grant had cracked down, took revenge by starting rumors of intemperance in camp, expecting and intending to take advantage of the troubles Grant had had before he left the Army seven years previously. Washburne expressed concern on the subject, which was promptly and decisively allayed by Rawlins, who reported that he had observed Grant and found him a "strict temperance man."

The one battle fought by Grant's Cairo command in 1861—one of only five serious engagements throughout the nation in that first year of watchful waiting and preparation—was the battle of Belmont. Early in November the Confederate forces at Columbus, Kentucky, had developed such strength that they threatened to aid the Rebels in Missouri, who still endangered the loyalists' control of that border state. Almost three thousand gray-clad men were encamped at Belmont, a tiny crossroads village across the river from Columbus. Grant led an equal number of men on transports, convoyed by two gunboats, down from Cairo to Belmont.

In this, his first real fight, his men initially dispersed the enemy troops and seized their camp. Then, raw, and intoxicated with victory, they behaved as if the war was over. Some listened to the officers make speeches, others looted and reveled. The enemy was reinforced, and the fleeing troops rallied and surrounded the careless victors. Grant, who at first had been unable to control his men, brought them to their senses by ordering the tents of the enemy set afire. When some of the Union men panicked and whined that they were surrounded and would have to surrender, he declared that they had cut their way in and they would cut their way out. The men successfully fought their way aboard their transports and Grant himself was one of the last to embark.

In the battle of Belmont losses in the two contending forces were about equal. From one technical point of view it was a Confederate victory, since they had retained possession of the field. However, the Union forces had not planned to seize and occupy the ground and could claim that it was at least a draw. The outcome was of value to the Union in preventing reinforcement of the Rebel troops in Missouri and discouraging offensive action against Cairo by the Columbus-based Confederates. Grant wrote his wife the day after the battle: "Taking into account the object of the expedition, the victory was most complete. It has given me a confidence in the officers and men of this command that will enable me to lead them in any future engagement without fear of the result."

12

The First Great Union Victory

★★★★

BRIGADIER GENERAL Ulysses S. Grant naturally could not help feeling a certain amount of satisfaction as he visited St. Louis early in 1862. There, three years before, he had been a man unable to support his family, in debt, and about to turn to his father and younger brothers for help. Now the proud and masterful leader of twenty thousand men, he could visit old friends with his head up and pay some of his old obligations. He visited his wife's family and found the slaveholding Dents more hospitable than he expected. For one thing, his classmate, Fred, Jr., had joined the Union army; for another, a general's uniform is a matter of family pride and prestige, even if it is the wrong color.

In one way the trip came close to being a disaster. Active in the rural neighborhood of the Dent plantation was a pro-slavery secret society known as the Knights of the Golden Circle. This was but one of the fifth-column movements, inspired by race prejudice and ideas of white supremacy, that flourished in the North and that beset the Lincoln Administration during the war. When a local group learned of Grant's return, they plotted to kidnap the Union general. One of its members, who had been a beneficiary of the ex-captain's compassion and generosity during the Hardscrabble years, sent him a warning, and he escaped by returning to St. Louis by a longer and different road.

The visit to St. Louis was not a pleasure trip, and while

he escaped discomfiture or worse in the country, Grant's official business in the city seemed to have failed. His purpose was to try to persuade Major General Henry W. Halleck, commander of Union forces in the West, to give him permission to pursue his plan to open a roadway to the South. Fort Henry was the Confederate strong point on the Tennessee River, just below the Kentucky border, which, with Fort Donelson on the Cumberland, a dozen miles away, Grant saw as guarding the gateway to the road he knew had to be opened for victory. Grant was impatient for action, was sure that his troops were ready, and had concluded on the basis of reports received in early January that the time had come to use his combined land and naval forces to attack. Halleck, a cautious and conservative student of military theory, cut Grant short before he had even finished explaining his plan. "Preposterous," said Halleck. "You can't do it with under sixty thousand men." After an interview of less than ten minutes, Grant was dismissed. He left St. Louis frustrated and crestfallen.

Within two weeks he tried again, making his request in writing. This time he had the help of a strong separate dispatch by Commodore Foote, commander of his river fleet. Halleck, who had learned meanwhile that the Confederate forces in the area were about to be reinforced, yielded and gave permission to attack Fort Henry, so that it could be taken before it was strengthened. Less than twenty-four hours later Grant began to embark fifteen thousand men on transports. On the following day the voyage began, under the convoy of seven of Foote's queer-looking gunboats–turtles, some called them–up the Ohio from Cairo, past Paducah, and then up the Tennessee. Smoke surged from the flotilla in black clouds, each riverboat burning raw pine under its boilers and looking, from a distance, like a house afire. "As far as the eye could see," a Confederate officer wrote, "the course of the river could be traced by the dense volumes of smoke."

A combined army and navy attack on Fort Henry had been planned, but flood conditions had weakened its defenders and the Union forces had not even reached their assigned point of attack when the fort surrendered to Foote, after an hour and a half of naval bombardment. After the troops pulled their boots out of the mud and occupied the place, Grant learned that most of the garrison had escaped to join and reinforce the Rebel troops at Donelson, eleven miles away. One of the Confederate officers who was left behind gave this picture:

> General Grant impressed me as a modest, amiable, kindhearted but resolute man. One of his officers came in to report that he had not found any papers giving information of our forces, and to save him further looking, I informed him that I had destroyed all papers bearing on the subject. "By what authority," he angrily demanded. Did I not know that I was laying myself open to punishment? Before I could reply, General Grant quietly broke in with "I would be much mortified and surprised if one of my subordinate officers should allow information which he could destroy to fall into the hands of the enemy."

Elated by the easy capture of Fort Henry and at the vindication of his plan, Grant gave the orders he had received a liberal interpretation, and though they did not mention an attack on Fort Donelson, he wired Halleck that he was moving on. He had learned that Donelson, barrier to the Cumberland River, as Henry had been to the Tennessee, was commanded by John B. Floyd, traitorous Secretary of War under President Buchanan, and Gideon Pillow, whom he well knew from his Mexican War service to be inept and a coward at heart. Grant took off with his men across the country between the rivers so quickly that he was not around when Halleck's return wire arrived, instructing him to stay at Henry and await reinforcements.

The battle for Donelson was not easy. The besieged outnumbered the besiegers. Grant's men deployed around the outer works of the fort to await the return of the gunboats, which were using the river network, just as Grant had always visualized, by steaming down the Tennessee, along the Ohio, and then back up the Cumberland. When the gunboats arrived, there began a furious bombardment, during which the boats approached too close to the fort and sustained serious damage, Foote himself being wounded. The next morning Grant visited Foote on board his flagship at the latter's request for a council of war. The general arrived wearing a battered old hat, the muddiest man in the army. He was chewing on a cigar, calm and unperturbed. His preliminary attacks on the fortress had not gone well, but he had not lost his confidence. He persuaded Foote to leave at least two of the gunboats rather than withdraw them all for refitting.

On that same morning, as Grant was meeting with Foote, the besieged troops had launched a heavy attack on the right of the Union line in a desperate attempt to break through. They had made progress after some hours, and signs of demoralization began to appear as the units under General McClernand began to give way. Pillow, however, did not have the ability or courage to follow through on his advantage, and while the Union line had swayed back, matters were at a momentary standstill. As Grant landed from Foote's ship, he heard the news and galloped to the point where the hardest fighting had occurred. He found confusion in his own ranks and a breakdown in the ammunition supply, which he quickly corrected. One of his men, discouraged and seeking to counsel retreat, told him that enemy prisoners had been found with knapsacks filled with rations. "They are prepared to fight three days; we can't go on!" he cried. Grant at once realized what no one else had, that the situation was the exact reverse: the only reason why soldiers emerging from a fortress would carry so much food would be that they were trying to escape.

"Some of our men are pretty badly demoralized," he said

to an aide, "but the enemy must be more so, for he has attempted to force his way out, but has fallen back; the one who attacks first now will be victorious and the enemy will have to be in a hurry if he is to get ahead of me."

He sent orders to his left wing to attack at once. Their leader was General C. F. Smith, who had been commandant of cadets at West Point when Grant studied there. Under his gallant leadership—he personally led the men into battle—they worked their way through the felled-tree obstacles and passed the outer line of the trenches guarding the fort and fought with such vigor that they were able to camp that night well inside the original Confedrate lines. Meanwhile McClernand's men, under Grant's inspiration, recovered their lost ground.

Within the fort that night there occurred a thoroughly ungallant and rather discreditable scene. Pillow and Floyd, with General Buckner, who had arrived with reinforcements, decided at a council that the fort must be surrendered. Floyd, under charges at Washington for stealing United States arms and munitions and turning them over to the enemy before the attack on Fort Sumter, feared that if captured he would be hanged for treason, and therefore he turned the Confederate command over to Pillow. The latter also feared, with less reason, that the Yankees were after his head, and turned the command over to Buckner. The latter sent over a flag of truce in the early morning hours, asking for the appointment of commissioners to discuss and agree on terms of capitulation. He proposed an armistice until noon for this purpose.

Grant sent back a reply that electrified the North and that has gone down in history: "No terms except an unconditional and immediate surrender can be accepted. I propose to move immediately upon your works." From these words, the initials of his name took on new meaning throughout the country: from every side and in every newspaper headline he became known as Unconditional Surrender Grant.

Grant met Buckner at the latter's headquarters in Dover Tavern, in the little Tennessee village nearby. The building is still maintained as a museum by the Fort Donelson Historical Society. Buckner reported that he was surrendering fifteen thousand men. The Union losses were 510 killed and 2400 wounded and missing. Since the national policy of emancipation was still a long way off, Grant permitted the Rebel officers to retain their orderlies; but he declined to permit the slaves who had labored on the fortifications to be returned to their masters.

This was the first time that Grant had seen Buckner since the latter had lent him fifty dollars when Grant was stranded in New York, penniless, eight years before. Grant took him quietly aside and offered his old friend the contents of his purse. They began to talk informally and at ease.

"Why did Pillow go?" asked Grant.

"He thought you'd rather get hold of him than any other," answered Buckner.

"Not at all," answered Grant. "If I'd caught him I would have let him go again. He would do us more good commanding you fellows."

"If I had been in command, you'd not have gotten up to Donelson as easily as you did," remarked Buckner. "If you'd been in command," answered Grant, "I would not have tried the way I did."

13

Mixed Rewards of Victory

★★★★

The capture of Fort Donelson was the first real victory for the Union forces in combat, after nine months of disillusioning and disheartening procrastination and defeat. Bells rang and bonfires blazed in all the cities of the North. The Rebel forces, whose greatest weakness was lack of industrial capacity, suffered a loss, immense to them, of infantry arms for twenty thousand troops and forty-eight cannon.

The psychological effect of the Union victory on the South was great. One Rebel officer recalled, "Dissatisfaction was general. Its mutterings, already heard, began to break out in denunciations. The demagogues took up the cry, and hounded one another and the people in hunting down a victim. The public press was loaded with abuse." General P. G. T. Beauregard, the captor of Fort Sumter, said the blows of Henry and Donelson "staggered the Confederacy; the demoralization of the army, the panic of the people, were complete."

Our newspapers often seem to thrive on sensational news and the Northern public devoured it. Grant, who had been practically unknown outside of Galena, St. Louis, and Cairo, became a national military idol overnight. His fame and popularity were enhanced by the words "unconditional surrender" in his message to General Buckner, and the phrase became a colorful rallying cry for the Union. Pictures of

Grant were in great demand. The report that he was holding an unlit cigar as he returned from visiting Commodore Foote resulted in hundreds of boxes of cigars being shipped to his headquarters from every point in the Union. Few of the sensation mongers and hero worshipers realized how much had been achieved by Grant in opening the Cumberland and Tennessee rivers by the victories of Fort Henry and Fort Donelson.

A vital hole had been punctured in the defenses of the Confederacy, and the Rebels lacked the forces to repair it. The basic defense line of the entire western Confederacy began to crumble all the way from the Appalachian Mountains to the Mississippi. The river routes to Nashville and to northern Alabama were opened and the Union dominance of the waters gained by the use of the "turtles" created a continuing threat to the rear of the Rebel positions at Columbus on the Mississippi and Bowling Green to the east. It became necessary to evacuate Columbus despite its almost impregnable fortifications. Nashville also had to be evacuated, a city which to the people west of the mountains meant as much as Richmond to the east. This was the result of the hard choice forced on the remaining Rebel commander in that area, Albert Sidney Johnston: whether to try to hold the Mississippi or middle Tennessee. He could not hold both, with Union naval forces dominating the Tennessee and Cumberland. Grant had created a rear, the one weakness that the Confederacy had not had at the start of the war.

In later years Grant declared his belief that Donelson's fall might have led to a speedy end of the war if the Union troops in that sector had been under unified and aggressive command so that those victories could be followed up before the Confederate forces regrouped and reformed. Unfortunately there was no single command; Grant was still a subordinate, and the commanders then in charge were too busy sending each other messages to seize the opportunity.

Other obstacles to pursuit arose. Success begets jealousy and national fame leads to envious criticism. Halleck, Grant's commander at St. Louis, was a man of bitter prejudices and distrusted Grant because of the stories of his drinking habits that had circulated in the Army eight years before and which the gossips were now peddling again. His attitude was not improved when he saw Grant receiving glory which he thought should have gone to him for the achievements of the troops under his over-all command.

At this particular juncture, due either to the sabotage of a traitorous telegraph operator or the confusion attendant on establishing communications from new positions, there was an interruption in the messages between Grant and Halleck. For a few days, each had been sending messages, which the other had not received. Not having received Halleck's orders to hold back and report the strength of his forces and avoid further engagements, Grant had moved on to Nashville, turned the city over to General Buell (who commanded a neighboring Union district) and was seeking to organize his forces for further pursuit, when he received an order to place General Smith in command and return to Fort Henry. The message complained inexplicably of a refusal to obey orders to report strength and positions of his forces.

This was followed by further criticism and, at a time when pursuit might have been of great value, Grant was placed on the sidelines. While this was going on, Halleck was intriguing against Grant in messages to Washington, but President Lincoln had been more impressed by Grant's victories than Halleck's gossip and demanded specific charges. At this point Halleck backed down and said that the "irregularities had been remedied" and restored Grant to command. "Instead of relieving you," he finally wired Grant, "I wish you, as soon as your new army is in the field, to assume immediate command, and lead it to new victories."

Meanwhile, however, Albert Sidney Johnston was withdrawing his temporarily demoralized Confederate forces unmolested to Murfreesboro. He was then able to swing over to the strategic rail center of Corinth in Mississippi and effect a junction with a reinforcing army under the command of Beauregard, which included the flower of New Orleans youth. By the time Grant resumed command the Southern forces were once more a menace and the opportunity to exploit the breakthrough was lost.

Grant bore the period of criticism and intrigue with dignity and restraint. After stating his defense to Halleck against the latter's complaints, he added, "If my course is not satisfactory, remove me at once. I do not wish in any way to impede the success of our arms. . . . My going to Nashville was strictly intended for the good of the service and not to gratify any desire of my own. Believing sincerely that I must have enemies between you and myself who are trying to impair my usefulness, I respectfully ask to be relieved from further duty in the department."

Shortly after having been restored to command, Grant wrote once more to Congressman Washburne, the man responsible for his first general's star, to whom, more than any other, he felt bound to account. He wanted to vindicate himself, he said, "not that I care one straw for what is said individually, but because you have taken so much interest in my welfare."

The criticism that had been voiced about his delay in messages to Halleck is brushed off as an afterthought at the end of the letter. The attack that gave him real concern, and about which he wanted to explain to Washburne, dealt with the slavery question. "I see by the papers," he said, "that I am charged with giving up a certain number of slaves captured at Fort Donelson. My published order on the occasion shows that citizens were not permitted to pass through our camps to look for their slaves." He went on then to explain that there were a few Negroes at Donelson who complained that they had been brought from Kentucky to work for officers, protested that they were free men, and wanted to get back to their families. "These I let go, and none others."

He closed this part of the letter with a statement that should be a classic. It concerned the relation of the military officer to the civilian government in a democracy. We have become accustomed to the idea that elevation in military rank is an achievement of sorts and sometimes listen to the political opinions of generals as though they were especially qualified to utter them. Grant gave in a few lines the answer to such pretension by military men of political qualifications:

> So long as I hold a commission in the army I have no views of my own to carry out. Whatever may be the orders of my superiors and law I will execute. No man can be efficient as a commander who sets his own notions above law and those whom he has sworn to obey. When Congress enacts anything too odious for me to execute, I will resign.

14

The Sad and Bloody Field of Shiloh

★★★★

GRANT REJOINED his army as soon as he was restored to command in mid-March. Most of his men had moved south along the Tennessee River, one of the two water-highways across the state of Tennessee that had been opened by the capture of Henry and Donelson. The principal encampment to which the Union troops had moved before Grant arrived was a field on a bluff, west of the stream, at Pittsburg Landing, one of the numerous local rural river stops out of which branched the muddy roads of the region. In the midst of the field was a little log church that bore the name Shiloh.

Less than thirty miles south and west of the Landing, across the Mississippi border, was the major railroad junction of Corinth. Because of its key location, and especially because of the presence there of the forces rallied together by Generals Albert Johnston and Beauregard, Corinth was the next objective. Grant placed General William T. Sherman in charge of the Shiloh camp, while he maintained army headquarters downriver at the little hamlet of Savannah on the other bank. There he awaited the arrival of another Union general, Buell, whose forces had been freed by the crumbling of the Confederate Kentucky line that followed the seizure of the river forts. When they united, the two armies were confidently expecting to march on Corinth.

For a brief period the main body of Grant's Army of the Tennessee remained encamped at Pittsburg Landing, while the general commuted daily from Savannah, where he awaited Buell's Army of the Ohio, and received and directed the disposition of the fresh untrained troops arriving to strengthen his own forces. Confederate General Johnston, however, instead of obligingly waiting to be attacked, marched over from Corinth in order to catch Grant before Buell's troops could arrive. Sherman, as commander at the camp, and Grant, as over-all commander, did not expect a full-scale attack. The Union forces at Shiloh field had not entrenched themselves and were not prepared for what was to follow.

On the morning of April 6, 1862, Johnston's army of forty thousand men came up to the Union lines undetected, incredible as it may seem to us now. They attacked on a broad front and brought on one of the fiercest and deadliest battles of the war. When the battle began the Confederate forces were larger, and they had the advantage of surprise. Some of the Union troops not only had never heard a gun fired in battle before, they had not even finished elementary drill. Some regiments broke and ran and stopped running only when they came to the river, where they cowered in the shelter of the river bank. The bulk of the Union forces fought bravely and held on with almost incredible tenacity against an attack that was itself unbelievably intense and courageous. The Union lines gave, and the Confederates pushed persistently forward.

Grant was at Savannah having breakfast when he first heard the firing at the front. He started at once on a boat for Pittsburg Landing. When he arrived, he quickly came to an estimate of the situation. From the many stragglers and fugitive soldiers at the river bank, the reports of panic-stricken line commanders, the noise and smoke of battle and the direction of the firing, it was quite apparent that the Union forces, still fighting bravely, were for the time being fighting a losing battle. Johnston's battle plan called for sweeping the Grant army into the river and destroying most of it, and he was coming perilously close to succeeding.

When Grant arrived and received the preliminary reports of the battle, he began at once to ride from one unit to another and to confer at each point with the regimental or division chiefs. Perhaps alone of all the leading Union officers, he declined to admit defeat or even the possibility of defeat. He moved regiments to new positions and gave orders for fresh supplies of ammunition to be moved up to the front. The most crucial fighting of the day, the defense of one point by an isolated group of two thousand men, long past the time when most officers would have surrendered, was the result of Grant's order and inspiration. General Prentiss and his men, who held out and checked the Rebel attack for long enough to keep it from engulfing the rest of the Union lines, fought so hard and so bitterly that their strong point has gone down in history as the "Hornet's Nest," so sharp and frequent were the stinging waves of bullets that emerged from their lines.

Grant never paused long at any particular place in the lines, spoke briefly and to the point at each, maintained throughout his even temper, always smoking his cigar. In all the wild combat he was completely imperturbable—as he had been at Fort Donelson. His commands were given in a low, penetrating, vibrant voice; he was constantly on the alert, yet completely undemonstrative. Expected reinforcements were delayed by fantastic misunderstandings; the lines wavered, but even though they held, they moved back, and a point was reached where the Confederates had taken all but one of the Union divisional headquarters.

Just as the Union reinforcements had been delayed by mishap, the greatest blow to the Confederate cause that day was struck by chance, when a Union bullet cut down General Albert Sidney Johnston, who was leading his men, in person, against a stubborn strong point. If Johnston had lived to continue the attack, the battle might have gone badly for the Union. As it was, General Beauregard, who took over the Confederate command, halted the attack for the day, believing that the battle was won and that the victory could be clinched the next morning.

It rained during the night and the troops, worn down almost beyond human endurance, had a miserable time. Grant, who had seemed so indifferent during the day to the death and wounding of thousands on both sides, could not bear the sight or sound of the injured in the shelter of the shanty where he had sought refuge. Sherman found him outside, sitting at the base of a tree, hat pulled down, coat collar turned up. Many have failed to understand the gift Grant had of being able to ignore, in the heat of battle, the suffering of his troops. That capacity to ignore suffering and to avoid panic in a crisis was a mark of his greatness, and a key to his ability to reduce the ultimate total amount of suffering that would be inflicted. The moment a battle was over, when it was no longer essential to be able to ignore pain and misery, Grant's compassionate nature responded more quickly and deeply than that of most officers.

By the morning of the second day the Union formations had been reinforced as some of Buell's troops appeared. A missing division of Grant's army arrived under the command of General Lew Wallace, who was to win more enduring fame as the author of *Ben-Hur* than as the leader who could not find the battlefield of Shiloh after marching all day from a camp five miles away. An assault was made at daybreak all along the line and the conditions of the previous day were reversed. The Rebels were steadily driven back, and by three o'clock they were in full retreat.

The battle came to an end when Grant decided against immediate pursuit. His men were exhausted and the roads were bad. Each side paused to count its casualties; in proportion to the war as it had been conducted so far, they were shocking, even frightful. Within a few days, as the sad messages arrived, there were many American homes, North and South, in mourning. George W. Cable, Louisiana writer, who fought as a young Confederate soldier and was later practically driven out of the South because of his stand for Civil Rights, said, "New Orleans was never glad again, after Shiloh." This was not to be the last time that the stubborn and heroic American soldier faced his brother in epic struggle, but the shock of its tragic toll has made this battle stand out in our national memory perhaps more than any other.

The battle of Shiloh buried the Rebel myth that one Southerner equaled five Yankees; it dispelled the hope that one good whipping was all the Confederates would need before they gave up and went home.

General Grant in his dispatch to headquarters, reporting on the battle, began in these words:

> It becomes my duty again to report another battle, fought by two great armies, one contending for the best government ever desired, and the other for its destruction. It is pleasant to record the success of the army contending for the former principle.

15

In and Out of Favor and Command

★★★★

"THE GREAT NUMBER of attacks made upon me by the press of the country is my apology for not writing to you oftener, not desiring to give any contradiction to them myself." So wrote Grant to Congressman Washburne in May of 1862, hardly a month after the retreat of Beauregard's troops from the battlefield of Shiloh. "I would scorn being my own defender against such attacks, except through the record. . . ."

Although the first aggressive campaign of the Confederates in the West had been frustrated at Shiloh, the battle won no honors for Grant, and he was once more under a cloud. His problem this time was not alone with Halleck, who arrived four days after the battle to take command in person; it was also with much of the press of the North. The first reports to reach the papers were those of hostile critics, some inspired by envious rivals. The shocking casualty lists created a strong temptation to find a scapegoat, and none could be a more logical candidate than the commanding officer. Men who had scattered to the rear at the sound of the first shots on Sunday morning sought excuses for their own delinquency and found fault with their general.

One reporter wrote, without any basis in fact, that Grant's "drunkenness or incompetency or both" had cost eight thousand Union lives at Shiloh. This was *The New York Times*! The Boston *Traveller* reported a "universal dislike (for

Grant) as a leader of men." The New York *World* accused him of an "imbecility which has no parallel in this war," and tried to coin a new nickname: "Ulysses *Surprise* Grant." It did not last very long.

As Grant's letter to Washburne shows, he lacked what we would call today a good sense of "public relations." Except for one letter, he stubbornly refused to speak in his own behalf. Nevertheless, he did not lack for defenders. One of the most outspoken and active was General William Tecumseh Sherman, for whom Shiloh was the beginning of a brotherly comradeship with Grant that lasted for the duration of the war and provided a basis for teamwork that played no little part in gaining the victory. It helped in answering congressional detractors that Sherman's brother was United States Senator from Ohio.

One newspaper correspondent who covered the Army of the Tennessee and traveled with Grant, reported: "He silently smoked and waited. The only protest I ever knew him to utter was to the correspondent of a journal that had denounced him with great severity. 'Your paper is very unjust to me, but time will make it all right.' "

Abraham Lincoln said, with the sure sense he had of the needs of the nation, "I can't spare this man, he fights." That put an end to the agitation to have Grant's head roll. But, outranked by Halleck, who had come to the front from the St. Louis armchair in which he had guided the war up till that time, Grant was denied the chance to lead his men in what might have been an important campaign that could have shortened the war.

Halleck resumed the trip to Corinth that was interrupted on the battlefield of Shiloh, but he was not in a great hurry. Cautious not to repeat the mistakes of the previous battle, he succeeded in making new ones. At a time when it was no longer necessary for his huge army to entrench, he entrenched every night. The army fairly crawled. When Grant suggested, "Why not press on to Vicksburg before it can be strengthened?" he was told, "When your advice is needed it will be asked."

The net result was, that after crawling very painfully from position to position for nearly two months, Halleck reached Corinth at the end of May to find that the Confederate army had departed. Halleck thought this was a great victory, but Grant knew better. He had learned at Shiloh that the South could not be conquered until its armies were destroyed and its resources gone.

Just as an opportunity to speed the end of the war had been lost by delay after the fall of Donelson, so again, the dawdling after Shiloh gave the Confederate forces time to recuperate, regroup, and retreat in good order through their own country. They were able to fortify Vicksburg more strongly and to recruit new troops for their army. Finally, after the occupation of Corinth, the Union forces were dispersed instead of concentrating on a single campaign, such as making the march to the Gulf of Mexico that Grant had envisioned.

As Halleck's second in command, Grant had as much authority as a musical comedy vice-president. He was not sulky or resentful, but chafed inwardly at the passing of a great opportunity that he would have known how to seize. He asked leave to be relieved from duty, and it was granted. He had made his preparations to depart, when Sherman heard of it and came to his quarters.

"Why are you going?" asked the red-bearded, impetuous Sherman.

"You know that I am in the way here," answered Grant. "I have stood it as long as I can."

"Where are you going?"

"To St. Louis," answered Grant, staring at the tent floor.

"Do you have any business there?" Sherman insisted.

When Grant admitted that he did not, that he just wanted to get away, Sherman argued pointedly that if he went the war would go on, just the same; that he would

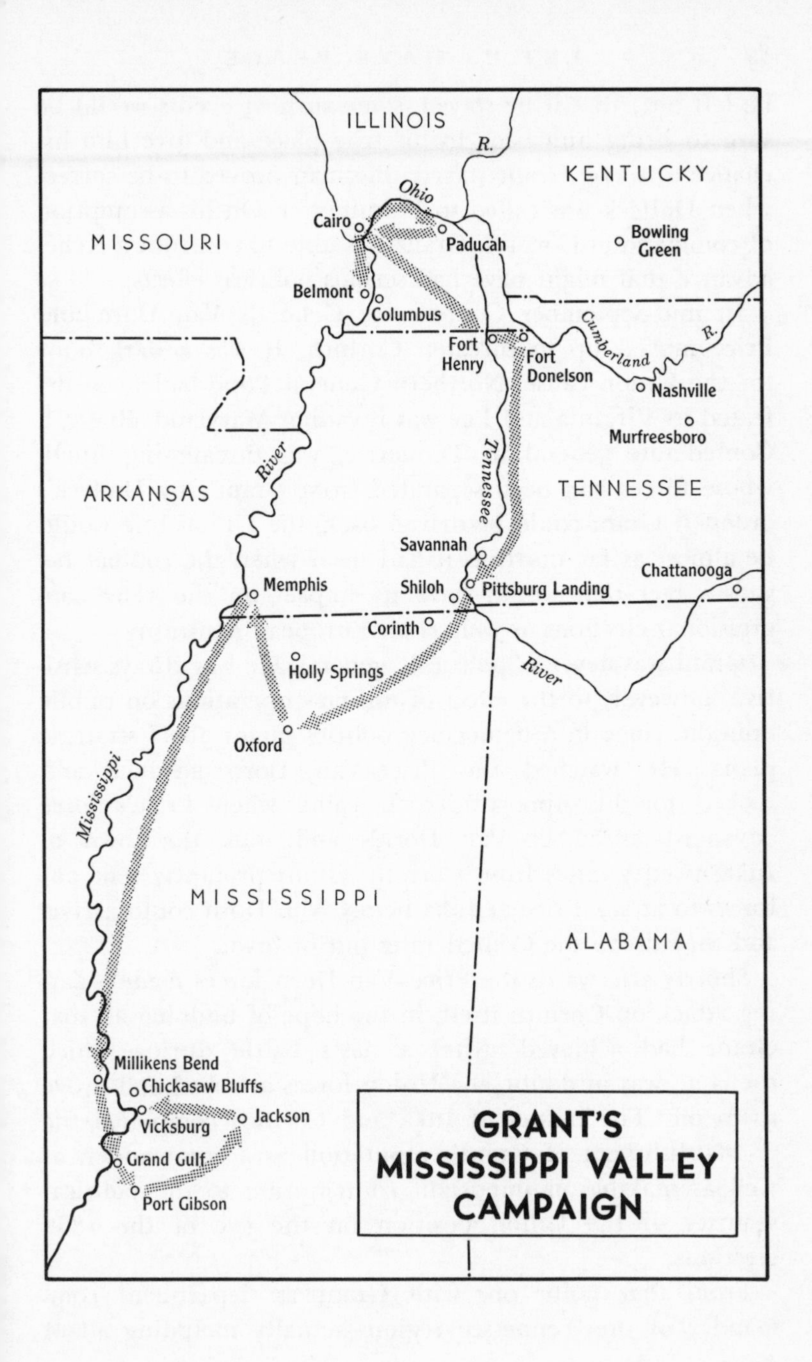
ILLINOIS
KENTUCKY
MISSOURI
Ohio
R.
Cairo
Paducah
Bowling Green
Belmont
Columbus
Fort Henry
Fort Donelson
Cumberland
R.
Nashville
Murfreesboro
River
Tennessee
ARKANSAS
TENNESSEE
Savannah
Chattanooga
Memphis
Shiloh
Pittsburg Landing
Corinth
Holly Springs
River
Oxford
Mississippi
MISSISSIPPI
ALABAMA
Millikens Bend
Chickasaw Bluffs
Vicksburg
Jackson
Grand Gulf
Port Gibson
GRANT'S MISSISSIPPI VALLEY CAMPAIGN

be left out; that if he stayed, some turn of events would be sure to bring him back to his true place and give him his chance to serve. Grant stayed. Sherman proved to be correct when Halleck was called to Washington. On his assumption of command at Corinth, Grant was able to confront a Rebel advance that might have had serious political effects.

In mid-September Confederate Generals Van Dorn and Price moved up to threaten Corinth. It was a dark hour for the Union cause. Northern General Pope had been defeated in Virginia and Lee was invading Maryland. Bragg, a Confederate general in Tennessee, was threatening Buell, whose forces had been separated from Grant's by Halleck's order. If Grant could be driven back, the Union line would be almost as far north as it had been when the conflict began—a fact that would have its impact on the 1862 congressional elections as well as on European neutrality.

Grant was never a "political" general. He was always sensitive, however, to the effect of military operations on public opinion, since in a democracy politics might affect strategic plans. He watched the Price–Van Dorn advance and looked for his opportunity. It came when Price's force advanced ahead of Van Dorn's and took the town of Iuka, twenty miles from Corinth. Grant promptly sent out forces to attack Price at Iuka before Van Dorn could arrive, and they drove the Confederates out of town.

Shortly afterwards the Price–Van Dorn forces made a daring attack on Corinth itself, in the hope of undoing all that Grant had achieved. After a day's battle during which the issue was in doubt, the Union forces attacked and drove them off. The battles of Iuka and Corinth completed the re-establishment of Grant's reputation as a commander, as well as making an important contribution to the political security of the Union position on the eve of the 1862 elections.

From that point on, with Grant as department commander of the Tennessee region—actually including all of the eastern Mississippi region—reinforcements began to swell his command and help strengthen it for the coming Vicksburg campaign, destined to be the most decisive of the war in the West.

16

The Dawn of Freedom

★★★★

FOR A LONG time the Union armies—the men, their officers, and the politicians who sent them in to battle—did not realize that they were fighting a war of liberation. They would have denied it if they had been asked and voted against it if they had had a choice. The belief that one race was better than another, that had been used to excuse the existence of slavery, had paralyzed the moral sense of many.

The Civil War ended slavery but it was not fought for that purpose, at first, by the Union forces. It was not until it was realized that slavery was not only the cause of the war but also the key to victory that the Union government accepted the idea of destroying it. On September 22, 1862—after having more than once reprimanded over-eager local commanders who had taken it upon themselves to proclaim freedom—President Lincoln, as an instrument of economic and psychological warfare, declared that all slaves in states remaining in rebellion would be declared, on January 1, 1863, "henceforward and forever free."

To the crusading abolitionists of the Northern states, who saw realized the dreams and hopes of thirty years, and to the political leaders in Washington who welcomed the announcement, freedom was only a word and the Emancipation Proclamation a scrap of paper which they had no power to enforce. It remained for Grant to be the first of the Union commanders to have the authority and the responsibility for dealing with freedom as a living thing, in a practical form, for large groups of men and women. As the commander who, after winning the battles of Iuka and Corinth, had occupied more slaveowning territory than all the other Union commanders put together, he faced the living embodiment of the "practical" problem that the antiabolitionist New England conservatives had worried about for years. How, they always would ask, could you handle the job of keeping communities going, when their whole economy had been based on slave labor; how could you suddenly change hundreds of thousands of men and women from a state of slavery to freedom overnight.

The problem was Grant's because as military commander of the occupied territory of Tennessee and northern Mississippi he was forced to handle problems of civil administration. He was not at all unprepared and had given the subject much thought in those long months when he was winning his reputation as an organizer and a trainer of men, then as a leader of regiments, divisions, and armies. During the summer of 1862, over a month before the Emancipation Proclamation, he had learned the great truth that the Southern Negroes knew, before the Yankee soldiers themselves knew it, that they were an army of liberation. He wrote his sister in mid-August that the slaves "are beginning to have ideas of their own; every time an expedition goes out many of them follow in the wake of the army and come into camp. I am using them as teamsters, hospital attendants, company cooks and so forth, thus saving soldiers to carry the musket."

His past politics as a slavery-tolerating Democrat were quickly cast aside as Grant learned from events. He not only saw the advantage, unusual for an invading army in hostile territory, of a surplus of laborers and servants; he had the benefit of the direct military utility of a friendly people. Most invading forces—in those pre-radar and pre-aviation days—would wander blind and helpless in country known inside and out to their enemy. The Union forces, however, had guides who cheerfully helped them through every foot of terrain, every path, hill, and hollow.

Grant would hear stories such as that of the *Tribune* war correspondent taken prisoner by the Rebels, who declared on regaining freedom after his escape:

> God bless the Negroes. . . . they were ever our firm, brave, unflinching friends. We never made an appeal to them they did not answer. They revealed a devotion and a spirit of self-sacrifice that was heroic. . . . They were ignorant, oppressed, enslaved; but they always cherished a simple and a beautiful faith in the cause of the Union and its ultimate triumph, and never abandoned or turned aside from a man who sought food or shelter on his way to Freedom.

Halleck in Missouri in 1862 had refused to let fugitive slaves enter his lines. Other Union generals—Buell, Burnside, Hooker, Thomas, and McClellan—warned their soldiers against receiving fugitive slaves, and even permitted enemy civilians to come and remove their "property." Grant never did.

As Grant's armies moved down the Mississippi Valley, it became more than a mere question of a few or a few dozen fugitive slaves. There was a massive swarming of the slaves into the Union lines, determined to seek freedom in the shelter of the ranks of the Northern armies. Wherever the Army marched, and in spite of all obstacles and dangers from sentries and pickets, there came the rising tide of slaves seeking freedom.

Of course such an influx constituted a nuisance to soldiers and a hazard to the security of the Army. It could not be ignored, nor evaded, nor forced back. It had to be handled in some constructive and imaginative way. Grant had heard of a regimental chaplain, serving with a brigade of Ohio troops under his command, who was a most uncommon officer. This was John Eaton, a New Hampshire man who had been educated at Thetford Academy, Vermont, and at Dartmouth College, while working on his family farm and teaching school during the winter to help pay his way. Eaton had been made, on graduation, principal of a public school in Cleveland and within two years was superintendent of schools of Toledo. While there, and achieving recognition for phenomenal organizing ability and willingness to try new ideas, young Eaton began to study for the ministry. He was a divinity-school student when the war started.

As an army chaplain Eaton had had his share of danger and adventure before his outfit joined Grant's command. He was twice captured by Confederate troops and released each time because of his office, the second time after having preached to the men in gray at their commander's request. Marching south with Grant's army after Shiloh and Corinth Eaton, as well as his fellow chaplains, had seen the rising tide of slaves and fugitives coming to the Union lines, and observed their pitiful condition and distress. The individual efforts he and his comrades made were not adequate to meet one-hundredth of the difficulties of the situation.

One night Eaton noticed that his fellow officers seemed to be having a private joke at his expense. They hinted at some incredibly huge task that was awaiting him. He went to the regimental office and found an order from Grant, putting him in charge of the fugitives that came into camp, to organize them into suitable companies for working, and to see that they were properly cared for. The order concluded with a direction to Eaton to report to Grant in person.

Chaplain Eaton had his doubts and misgivings that November night in 1862 as he traveled to the little Tennessee town of LaGrange to meet his commanding general. He feared that he faced an impossible undertaking, doomed to bring him only disappointment and failure. He was not encouraged as he saw along the dusty road he traveled the groups of men, women, and children, some clad in rags or worse, some crudely bandaged where thorns or dogs had torn at them as they made their way to freedom. They had never tasted this freedom and knew not what it meant, yet their human instincts made them grasp it as they saw it come near.

Eaton regretted, too, having to leave his work as chaplain, where he knew he was needed for much more than mere leadership in prayer. There were the sick soldiers to be visited and the correspondence with the families of the dead and wounded. He made up his mind to appeal with all his energy for his release from the duty which, as a soldier, he could not refuse to undertake.

He dismounted and hitched his horse in front of the large house that had been pointed out to him as headquarters. The sentry directed him to enter, and walking up a hallway, he found an orderly in front of a door, who said, "Tap at the door and he'll tell you to come in." This was less ceremony than Eaton had ever seen at any headquarters before. He knocked, a voice said quietly, "Come in," and he found himself alone with Ulysses S. Grant. Eaton had read the unpleasant rumors that were especially widely peddled after the battle of Shiloh, and looked for signs of dissipation; he found none, and saw instead moderation and simplicity.

Though Grant was in the midst of preparations for what was to be his longest and most difficult campaign, he devoted much time then and afterwards to long, earnest conferences with Eaton about the problem of the freedmen. The very first exchange had to do with Eaton's effort to be relieved of the assignment. He mentioned the shortage of chaplains in his brigade; his inability, not having rank, to enforce the necessary orders; his possible conflict with cotton speculators and the like if he were to put the refugees to work in the fields. All that he said had no more effect on the quiet, attentive face of the General than a speech to a stone wall. At the conclusion Grant said simply:

"Mr. Eaton, I have ordered you to report to me in person and I will take care of you."

There followed a long, intensely interesting talk on the Negro problem—a problem which had hardly been faced as yet by the national Government in Washington. One aspect of its complexity was the many Union men from the border states who were slaveholders. The question was difficult, but Grant, who had himself owned a slave until less than two years before the war, was ready to act boldly. He told Eaton that the conditions that threatened his army—the multitude of refugees, hungry and unsheltered—would become aggravated as the troops advanced still further into the heart of the great slave population. He could not evade these problems, even if Congress had, until then. He told Eaton it was necessary to exercise some form of guardianship over them.

"How can all this be done?" asked Eaton.

"There are many ways," answered Grant. "The first thing to do is to set up a camp at Grand Junction. There the local residents distrusted us so much that they have provided us with empty homes and public buildings. Then you must organize work companies and see about the crops that have been abandoned in the fields."

"What can we, as an army, do with raw cotton?" asked Eaton.

"There's no law that says we can't sell it for the benefit of these people—and the ones who can't work, too," answered Grant quickly. "I tell you, Eaton, I have been thinking about this for a long time. I think that when the Negro proves himself as an independent laborer for hire—and I'm confident he can—it will be very easy to put a musket in his hand and make a soldier of him. If he fights well, you can put a ballot in his hand and make him a citizen!"

Eaton looked at Grant with new respect. He, the New England antislavery man, had not yet reached this point in his own thinking about the future. Nowhere else, in those days before the Emancipation Proclamation became a reality, had he heard the problem of the future of the Negro handled so vigorously and with such humanity combined with practical good sense.

17

Solutions and Problems

★★★★

THE SOLUTION was neither quick nor simple nor perfect. It could not be for a problem that was the result of many years of history. The first camp for the men who were not quite free and yet were no longer slaves was a group of deserted houses four or five miles from the principal army post. Old tents were used to round out the facilities when the houses were not enough. An initial burden was the need to locate and separate and provide for the care of the sick, of whom there were many. Nothing promotes the spread of illness and disease like poverty.

Even among those who were well, many were so broken in spirit that it was difficult to arouse them to a point where they could help themselves. Assistants were hard to get. In the ranks of the Union forces where volunteers were to be sought, the men had come to agree after what they had seen of the country and its people that slavery was evil and had to be destroyed; yet so strongly permeated were they with the racial feeling that whites were better than blacks that they would not offer to assist in helping the downtrodden to help themselves.

New and difficult problems were constantly arising. Eaton went to confer almost daily with General Grant, who kept his word and was always available to talk over or offer a solution for each new problem. He directed the quartermasters to issue such amounts of army rations as Eaton should requisition. He directed that clothing for men, women, and children be furnished. He took the first necessary step for putting his idea to work by ordering that Eaton be supplied with tools of all sorts, and particularly materials for baling cotton. It was cotton that had chained the men and women and children who had fled by the thousands to Grant's tents; he intended that cotton should help to free them.

Making these decisions involved a certain amount of risk for Grant. The troubles after the fall of Fort Donelson, the wave of attacks after Shiloh, were still fresh and he knew he was not immune to the intriguing of jealous officers and some politicians who hoped to end the war and restore the Union—on the slaveholders' terms. Long afterwards Grant once said to Eaton, "I wonder if you ever realized how easily they could have had our heads!"

The camp at Grand Junction soon began to assume some order and to give promise of achieving their aims. It was too late to plant a new crop, but there was much of the abandoned 1862 crop to be salvaged. Squads of Negro men and women under the protection of soldiers began to go out into the deserted fields of the Confederate planters and gather the corn and cotton. Within a very short time each camp came to be organized on the basis of a cooperative community, with the wage rates fixed by the men assisting Eaton, and the proceeds being pooled for the benefit of all—the sick, the aged, and the young.

Those farmers and planters who had not fled in panic as the army of liberation approached naturally found that their slaves were no longer content to carry their burden on the old basis. For the benefit of those willing to cooperate, Eaton, with the permission of Grant, intervened. If they would pay wages to their field workers, on the same level as that fixed by the Union-sponsored camps, their ex-slaves would be encouraged to work for them.

So successful was the first six weeks' experience that Grant extended Eaton's authority and established official regulations for the conduct of his office. Most important of all, Eaton was granted authority to request the assignment of men from the army units in the vicinity to aid in the work which up to then their prejudices, or fear of the prejudices of their comrades, had kept them from volunteering to do.

The freedmen in Grant's territory became self-sustaining; the cotton and corn that might have been lost was salvaged. They learned the obligations as well as the rights of citizenship. When the crops were gathered, and before the time for new planting had arrived, they were engaged in cutting wood along the Mississippi to supply the large number of steamers operating there—the lifeline and a chief source of the military superiority of the national forces in the region. The woodcutting efforts of the freedmen enabled thousands of Union soldiers who might otherwise have had to be detailed for this work to keep up the pressure on the foe. At the same time, the money paid by the Government for the wood, as Grant wrote later, created a fund "not only sufficient to feed and clothe all, old and young, male and female, but to build them comfortable cabins, hospitals for the sick, and to supply them with many comforts they had never known before."

Of course there were more than physical needs to be met. During their bondage the ex-slaves had not only not received any education; they had been forbidden by law to learn to read or write. Now that they could lift their heads they were hungry to learn. All over the South this characteristic of these people was noted; when they were later to be permitted to fight for the freedom of their land, they were often seen in the rifle pits with a speller in one hand and a musket in the other. To their aid came many devoted men and women from the North, whose trips were financed by Freedmen's Aid Societies that sprang up in every region. These offered their services as teachers or in any form of practical philanthropy in which they should prove to be useful. Representatives of what were then called the "best" families, as well as people of all walks of life, sacrificed all the comfort and security of their homes and devoted themselves under the most difficult circumstances to the work of improving the condition of the Negro. Their reward, when the war was over, was to be ostracized and driven out of the communities to which they had come to help; on top of that they were to be lied about in many history books and given the hateful name of "carpetbaggers."

One day while visiting Oxford, Mississippi, Chaplain Eaton met old Jesse Grant, who had come down with Julia to visit his son. Jesse returned to Grand Junction with Eaton and filled him with anecdotes. One of the most revealing stories that Jesse told went back to a day early in the war when Jesse was still full of thoughts of his recent leather and hide business, and came to the scenes of the war with a tanner's point of view. As he saw the waste of hides on the route of the army and at the slaughter camps he was filled with dismay. He approached his son, but no sooner had he opened his mouth on the subject than Lys told him that he would not permit him to make use of the hides in any way; he would not permit his army office to become a source of profit to anyone with whom he had any connection.

War brings with it many pressures and many temptations to grasping men. For two years Europe and the North had suffered because the largest single supply of cotton for their mills was cut off. At the same time that Grant's army was entering the area where the slaves swarmed forward, he was entering the richest cotton farming area in the South, the Mississippi Delta. Traders and speculators competed with each other for permits to come and buy the portions of the cotton crop that had been salvaged by the freedmen or harvested by the planters who did not flee.

The winter of 1862–63 was one of the most difficult for the Union forces. Grant faced the campaign for Vicksburg with an army weakened by Halleck's splinter tactics, knowing he opposed an enemy strengthened by Halleck's delays. His military problems of supply and organization were not made easier by the social problems of the freedmen that fell on his shoulders. The conniving of the speculators and traders who looked for favors in connection with cotton trading exasperated him, particularly when he learned that some of them had attempted to use his father's influence as a means of advancing their commercial interests.

Grant made a serious error, under the pressure of his combined problems, and he regretted it soon afterwards. He had become aware that some of the speculators and traders who had attempted to influence him or bribe officials serving under him were Jewish. He reacted angrily and issued an order condemning "the Jews as a class," and directing that all Jews be expelled from his department within twenty-four hours.

Whatever the provocation may have been, this harsh and discriminatory edict was entirely indefensible. Neither then nor ever could a whole group of people be fairly condemned or punished for the offenses of some of them. It does not free Grant's record from the stain which this act left on it to say that his intention was merely to solve the problem of speculation and influence-peddling rather than to persecute people for their race or their religion. Nor does it make his drastic order more defensible to say that because Jews were forbidden to engage in many occupations in European countries from which they had emigrated, they tended more often to be identified as traders in nineteenth-century America.

The obnoxious order did not remain in force very long, and whatever harm it did was soon remedied. Telegrams were sent by some of the residents affected and visits made to President Lincoln and Secretary of War Stanton. They would not believe, at first, that such an extraordinary and unfair action had been taken. When the President was convinced by being shown an official printed copy, he countermanded it at once and instructed General Halleck to order Grant to inform all post commanders that the order had been revoked and was no longer in effect. "To condemn a class," said Lincoln to a group that called on him, "is to wrong the good with the bad. I do not like to hear a class or nationality condemned on account of a few sinners."

The whole affair lasted less than two weeks. President Lincoln never thought it necessary to condemn Grant publicly for issuing the improper order. The President's opponents in Congress introduced a resolution denouncing Grant's order as "illegal, tyrannical, cruel, and unjust." This was an act of sheer hypocrisy, done for the purpose of taking a "poke at the administration," as one Jewish commentator has said, by censuring "the only general who seemed to be able to win battles."

The antislavery senators saw this and voted the resolution down. The wrong that Grant had done had been corrected by Lincoln, and the subject was closed. One of the majority declared in the debate, "It is wrong to single out any particular class of men in this country and as a class condemn them." However, since the principle they believed in had been established by Lincoln, and since Grant was the nation's instrument in fighting for a broad principle of human freedom, they rejected the attempt of the opponents of that broader principle to hamper the war effort by a formal vote of censure.

Grant was free, without further embarrassment, to go on with his campaign for Vicksburg.

18

Working Toward Vicksburg

★★★★

IN A WAR between two regions, through both of which runs one great river, control of that river is of prime importance. The blocking of the Mississippi denied a natural outlet to market to the farm and factory products of the Northwest. This increased the determination of the men of those parts to restore the Union.

The river provided countless jumping-off points for attack on a Confederate rear—a rear that did not exist when the war began. To divide the Confederacy was the most important military objective, since Texas, Arkansas, and most of Louisiana lay west of the stream and were an important source of food, military supplies, and recruits for the Rebel armies. Moreover Texas, with its border on Mexico, was a hole in the Union blockade of the southern coast through which quantities of cotton could be shipped out and contraband articles of war imported.

Grant had foreseen this early in the war, and his plans from the moment he was placed in command at Cairo were shaped in the direction of slicing down the Mississippi. Step by step he won, or made it possible for others to win, the strong points along the river—from the day that he took Fort Henry until the battle of Shiloh, when the forces drawn off from the defense of New Orleans made it possible for General Butler and Admiral Farragut to capture that great city. Now, in the early winter of 1862, the only remaining Rebel-held portion of the Mississippi lay between Vicksburg in the state of Mississippi and Port Hudson in northern Louisiana. That stretch of several hundred miles was almost as important to the South as the entire river had been. The stream of commerce and supply north and south along the river was blocked; the most important pathway to Arkansas and Texas, through Vicksburg itself, was kept open.

Of all the great rivers in the world, the Mississippi, especially its lower portion, is probably the most crooked. It is often necessary to sail thirty miles to travel between two points that are ten miles or less apart by land. The curves of the river are by no means fixed, however; it does not traverse a permanent rocky bed but cuts its way through soft soil in which it can make new channels overnight at the slightest pretext or on the occurrence of an unexpected obstacle. Thus, along its course there are numerous swampy islands and peninsulas, and along either side stagnant lakes, the remnant of former channels, and a network of sluggish tributary streams called bayous, these as crooked as the river itself. The country through which the bayous flow is filled with swamps and dense forests, and where there is dry ground, it is often covered with tangled masses of creeping vines. Not easy country, this, through which to lead an army.

At certain points along the river there were exceptions. On the eastern shore of the river the land terminates in high bluffs that run along its edge intermittently. Columbus, Kentucky, and Memphis, Tennessee, were strong points situated on such bluffs, which had fallen into loyal hands without battle as Grant outflanked (the military language for "got behind") them on his journey down the Tennessee River. Where there were no such bluffs, the Union fleet could dominate the banks of the stream and hold off the hostile forces. Vicksburg became the Gibraltar of the Confederacy because of its situation on the first high land coming to the edge of the river below Memphis. To the fleet it was inaccessible; to the army, nearly so. Access from the river, below Vicksburg, was cut off by swampy ground. Above the city, the height on which it was situated terminated at a point called Haines' Bluff, which was strongly fortified. The batteries defending Vicksburg from the riverside had been built by engineer officers trained in the U.S. Army Corps of Engineers, and were perfectly adapted to resist attack from the water.

The method that Grant had used in moving south prior to the Vicksburg campaign was no longer available to him. The Tennessee River turned east in the neighborhood of Corinth, and the relatively easier route of transport south by water could not be used. He began, however, by making an effort to travel along the route of a rail line heading south in the direction of Jackson, Mississippi. That city, his first objective, was situated on dry ground and almost due east of Vicksburg. His initial plan was to proceed along that line, while Sherman was to move south from Memphis along the river, and one or the other would keep moving, depending on which would attract the attention of the defending army under Confederate General Pemberton.

Grant and his forces had traveled about half the distance south, and his headquarters had reached Oxford, Mississippi, when there were two disastrous setbacks. Confederate General Forrest, a former slave trader, and now a roving cavalryman, swept north across the railroad down which Grant had traveled, destroying much track and so much telegraph wire that Grant was out of touch with both Sherman and Washington. That was followed by the raid of Rebel General Van Dorn on Holly Springs, Mississippi, where Grant had established an important supply base. A great quantity of food and ammunition, valued at $1,550,000 had been moved there and stored for the support of the southward-advancing Union army. The place was commanded by a Colonel Murphy, whom Grant had warned of the danger of raiders, and whom he had told that the only defense was to hold out at all costs—and that help would arrive in time. At daybreak of December 20, despite his having received Grant's order, Murphy was not only taken bu surprise, but he surrendered the town, his entire force, and all the valuable supplies with hardly a show of resistance. For this shameful conduct he was dismissed from the service.

Unwilling to wage a campaign without a base of supply, Grant was forced to retreat to Memphis, back to where his troops had started. He sent a message to Sherman, who was about to attack the bluffs above Vicksburg from the river. The wires having been cut by Forrest's raid, he was unable to head off Sherman. On December 29 Sherman's men attacked at Chickasaw Bluffs, five miles north of Vicksburg, and were driven back.

It was now midwinter, and nothing had been gained since autumn except experience. Meanwhile these disappointments in the West, together with defeats in the East, contributed to a new period of pessimism and defeatism among the people of the North. The only military consolation during the period was an inconclusive Union victory in Tennessee, the battle of Stone River, which was won, it was believed, because the Confederate Commander of Eastern Tennessee, Braxton Bragg, was forced by Grant to reduce his forces to send help to General Pemberton, the commander at Vicksburg.

There was a close call for the Grant family at Holly Springs. As Van Dorn's soldiers plundered and burned the loot that they could not carry with them, they destroyed Julia Grant's carriage and took her horses. Only the day before that Julia had left the town, after pausing to leave her carriage and much of her baggage, on her way to visit with Ulysses at the front.

With her as she traveled through the danger zone was their youngest child, four-year-old Jesse Grant. This was not the first time that one of the Grant family passed through peril during the conflict, nor was it to be the last. But Julia Grant had remembered from the very beginning of the war what a devoted father and husband Ulysses was and how much it meant to him to see her and one or more of the children as often as he could. She was glad to take the risks that come with being the wife of a commander. She and her husband knew, too, that as far as the children were concerned, except when the tide of battle might change swiftly and unexpectedly, there was not much more risk at the commander's tent or headquarters than there would be in many border places—such as Covington or St. Louis, where the family homes and connections had been in the period just before the war began.

At the very beginning of his career, when Ulysses took his first unruly regiment out from Camp Yates at Springfield, Illinois, and across the contested border state of Missouri for both training and defense, Fred, the eldest son, went along. When orders came to move into battle at Quincy, Ulysses wrote that he would send Fred—then eleven—home, and Julia wrote back immediately, urging him to let the boy stay with him. But Fred was already on the Mississippi, en route to Galena via Dubuque, and quite disgusted at what he was going to miss.

After the battle of Belmont, Ulysses sent for Julia and the three boys to come and stay in Cairo, which they did until the first major Tennessee campaigns began. Then she returned to Covington to stay with Jesse and Hannah and give the children a chance at school until the summer. To reach the Kentucky town, she had to disembark in Cincinnati, and there she hired a Negro hackman to take the family over the river to Jesse's. When the driver boarded the boat to return to Ohio, he was arrested, under a law forbidding a Negro to enter the state without a pass, and old Jesse bailed the man out, muttering and cursing at the injustices that still prevailed in so-called free territory.

Shortly after Fort Donelson fell, Ulysses wrote Julia of his wish—unfortunately to be frustrated—to move on as rapidly as possible, "to save hard fighting" later on. "These terrible battles are very good things to read about to persons who have lost no friends," he wrote, "but I am decidedly in favor of having as little of it as possible." He ended, "Kiss the children for me and the same for yourself." A couple of months later, during Halleck's slow march to Corinth, Grant remarked to a newspaper correspondent, "After the war is over —and I wish it might be over soon—I want to go back to Galena to live. I am saving my money from my pay now and I shall be able to educate my children."

When Halleck was called to Washington in July, and Grant once more took command of his army, Julia and the children joined him again. The grandparents did not approve, and the tone of one of Jesse's letters to his son during the summer can be seen from Lys's answer to his father.

> Your uneasiness about the influence surrounding the children here is unnecessary. On the contrary it is good. They are not running around camp among all sorts of people, but we are keeping house, on the property of a truly loyal secessionist who has been furnished free lodging and board at Alton, Illinois; here the children see nothing but the greatest propriety.

19

Victor at Vicksburg

★★★★

THE WINTER OF 1862–63 was a bad one for morale in the free states. The war news from Virginia was a chronic story of halfhearted advance followed by defeat, and unpleasant news from the Mississippi Valley was hard to take. When Grant's loss of supplies at Holly Springs was followed by Sherman's repulse at Chickasaw Bluffs, north of Vicksburg, the fickle press began to carp and criticize, as they had after Shiloh. One group of politicians went to President Lincoln and demanded Grant's removal. Lincoln answered calmly, "I rather like the man. Let's try him a little longer."

Grant was not one to be discouraged by defeat or disturbed by hostile press coverage. He had a calm confidence in himself; he knew his duty, and devoted himself to doing it. He realized that conditions in midwinter were not right for the plan of attack he had begun to develop in his mind. To overcome the geographical advantages and numerical superiority of the defenders of Vicksburg required waiting until spring. In that frequently water-logged area, spring was not a time of good roads and hard ground, but it was at least less muddy than winter.

Yet action was needed constantly, despite all the disadvantages of a wet Mississippi winter, and for two reasons. In the first place, it was essential to keep the troops active and on fighting edge, to season and toughen them. In the second place, morale in the loyal states required news of action to make up for the stalemate between the two great armies in Virginia.

The next phase of the Vicksburg campaign was marked by a variety of ingenious schemes, all directed at the achievement of two aims: the first, to get the Union gunboats and transports south of the batteries on the Vicksburg bluffs; the second, to get the Union Army onto the high and dry ground east of the town—the only direction from which it could be attacked without the perils that caused Sherman to be defeated at Chickasaw Bluffs. Typical of these schemes was Grant's canal. If the canal had been completed, ships and men would not have had to pass around the hairpin curve on which Vicksburg was situated but could by-pass the town, land to the south, and attack it from the rear.

Four thousand men worked on the canal, but by late winter all they had to show for it was the toughening up that came from exercise. A sudden rise in the river in March flooded the area surrounding the canal and destroyed much that had been done. Other attempts were meanwhile started to chart and pursue devious routes through the bayous, that might enable men and supplies to reach the target area. Some were beaten back and others had not progressed sufficiently to go on to completion when spring drew near, and Grant decided to call in and concentrate his forces for the campaign he had planned all along.

The real Vicksburg campaign that was to break the Confederacy and make Grant an unshakable popular hero did not begin until the end of March. All that had gone before, the canal-digging and the bayou-skirmishing, had served to pass the winter and toughen the army, but now real fighting weather had come. Grant's plan emerged: it was to march his army south of Vicksburg on the west side of the river, to run the Union fleet past the guns of the batteries on the bluffs to meet the troops, and to ferry the troops back across the river to the area south of their objective and close in.

Every one of Grant's generals was worried by the course that their leader had planned. To put his army south of

Vicksburg and then march up to the east of the city would mean having a Gibraltar-like fortress between their men and their base of supplies. Even more did the generals question the next move—crossing the river and plunging into the heart of enemy country. The bold and dashing Sherman was aghast and protested, "You will be putting yourself voluntarily into a position in which an enemy would be glad to maneuver a year to get you."

Sherman actually went on to put his protest into writing. In proper military style he handed the written protest to Grant, who by then had become his friend as well as his commander. "You will get my hearty cooperation in this movement," he said, as he handed the paper to Grant, "but I feel it due to my military reputation to protest against it in writing and request that it be forwarded to Washington through channels." Grant was not disturbed. "Very well, Sherman, send your protest along," he said.

The first move in Grant's campaign was the transfer of the bulk of his forces, which had been concentrated north of Vicksburg at Milliken's Bend, to a point on the west side of the river well south of the enemy fortress. The significance of this step was masked from the Rebel commander, Pemberton, by two diversionary attacks. One was a pretended foray by Sherman above Vicksburg, drawing there the attention of the forces in the town. The other was a daring and successful cavalry raid by Colonel B. H. Grierson, who moved with one thousand horsemen from southwestern Tennessee and across the state of Mississippi, spreading havoc and consternation, and destroying supplies and communications as he went, and finished up safely in Louisiana to the south. Most of that state was now held by Union forces that had advanced from New Orleans.

As the main body of Grant's troops was moving downriver, the Union fleet was preparing for one of the great naval gambles of the war. Clustered north of Vicksburg at Milliken's Bend, the fleet prepared to run the gauntlet of the batteries on the high bluffs and rendezvous with Grant below the town. Admiral Porter assembled seven of his ironclad "turtles" with three transports, each with the burden and protection of a loaded barge lashed to the port or fortress side. Shortly after midnight, April 15, 1863, Rebel pickets patrolling in rowboats sighted the convoy coming down the north leg of the hairpin turn of the river, on which the city stood. Suddenly there was a flare, then a rocket, then the whole river was lit up by houses which the Rebels had planned to burn whenever such an emergency arose. Each of the heavy guns on the cliffs started to pour shot and shell at the ships below. Each gunboat returned the fire as she passed the town, and men aboard could hear the clatter of falling bricks as houses crumpled under a hit. Every ship in the convoy was damaged; some went out of control and revolved helplessly in the river current until steering gear could be repaired. Despite the furious bombardment, however, every one got through, and Grant's first objective was attained when the convoy joined the troops that had marched south to a point opposite the fortified hamlet of Grand Gulf, the Vicksburg defenders' southernmost post.

The initial plan was to bombard Grand Gulf thoroughly, to land an expeditionary force, and march along a road that was known to lead inland. However, the Grand Gulf defenses would not be silenced, and a new landing point had to be found. As Grant pondered the problem, a local Negro proved once more the importance of these neighborhood allies in the fight for their own freedom. He had, from his hiding place in the fields, analyzed Grant's problem and come to headquarters.

"No need to go further down the river, General," he said when he was brought, at his own request, to the commander's tent. "You can cross at Bruinsberg."

"What about the roads?" asked Grant. "I need a high, dry road inland."

"Road's all right," said the Negro calmly. "I been over it many a time."

The road was not on Grant's maps, but the man looked, and was, reliable—as had been many of his race that the Union armies had encountered before. Unopposed, the army crossed the river that had frustrated them for months. The road inland led to a crossroads town, Port Gibson, where Grant's men fought and won the first battle of the final phase of the Vicksburg campaign. This victory forced the evacuation of Grand Gulf and set the stage for the series of maneuvers that were to lead to his most sensational victory.

One more difficulty arose at this point. Grant had expected to maintain himself at Grand Gulf for a period, while part of his men joined with troops of General Banks, New Orleans commander, in attacking and taking Port Hudson, the only other Confederate strong point on the Mississippi. Word was received that Banks would be delayed several weeks. Grant quickly decided to go it alone and head straight for Vicksburg. The enemy had been surprised by his landing, defeated at Port Gibson, routed from Grand Gulf, and was still off balance. Delay would enable them to recuperate and reinforce Vicksburg.

Grant made the boldest decision of the war. He smiled to himself in quiet satisfaction as he thought of how Halleck, now at Washington, would have ordered him back if he had known what he was up to. He knew that he was outnumbered by the defenders of the fortress city, but that they were scattered all over the landscape, fearfully waiting for him. He heard that a new enemy force was being gathered under Joseph Johnston—brother of the Albert Sidney who almost won at Shiloh—and that if Johnston joined forces with Pemberton the Vicksburg defenders might defeat him or hold him off indefinitely. He gave orders to march. The army started out in the direction of Jackson, ready at the drop of a hat to wheel over to Vicksburg. To get every available man into the march, no rearguard or watch on supply lines was maintained. He cut loose from his base of supplies, just as Winfield Scott had on the road to Mexico City. He had no rear.

In a series of rapid movements, hitting in each case where he was never expected to be, Grant thrust first at Jackson, took the town and drove off Johnston. Then he swung over at Vicksburg's defenders and fought two battles with them, beating them each time, and almost swinging around to outrace them to their own fortifications. Five successful battles were fought in eighteen days by his army on the march—with three days' rations in their knapsacks. For the rest, they lived off the country. Spattered with mud, his clothes worn and stained, Grant was constantly on the move up and down his lines, and wherever he appeared he was cheered by his men and in return brought renewed spirit to them. They all appreciated, as one of them wrote later, that "he meant business and spared himself not at all, and neglected no detail" for their efficiency, safety, or sustenance.

The weakened defenders of the fortress were driven back and gained their line of trenches and fortifications. Here they took their stand, although by now they were doomed. The Union men settled down grimly for one of the most famous sieges of modern military history. As Union reinforcements arrived, a vise slowly tightened around the city's supply lines. The river, the swamps, the bayous, and the bluffs, previously the shield of Vicksburg, now helped to strangle her. Two frontal attacks on the fortifications failed, and Grant and his men settled down for the long pull.

One day as Ulysses Grant was riding around his lines he stopped for water at a house in which a Rebel woman continued to live. Like most of her neighbors, she had been taught to hate the Yankees and would taunt them when she could. Recognizing Grant, and knowing that his army for the moment was stalled, she asked, "Do you ever expect to get into Vicksburg, General?"

"Certainly," he replied, quietly but firmly.

"I wonder when!" she remarked, with a sneer creeping up to the corners of her mouth.

"I cannot tell exactly *when* I shall take the town," quietly answered Grant, even more firmly, "*but I mean to stay here until I do if it takes me thirty years.*"

It did not take that long. On July 4, 1863, in one of the great coincidences of history, as Lee reeled back, beaten, from Gettysburg, Pemberton surrendered Vicksburg. Grant broke his own record, established at Donelson, for number of prisoners taken in one battle.

Toward the end he was conferring with Sherman on some military business, when an aide came and asked him for a document he was supposed to have. One of Grant's habits was to have the pockets of his uniforms stuffed with orders, maps, memoranda, and messages he had received. After he had found the paper the adjutant wanted, he took another out of the same pocket and handed it to Sherman with a smile. "Here is something that will interest you, that I always felt you would want back," he declared.

Sherman took the paper and opened it. It was the written protest against the Vicksburg campaign that he had handed to Grant weeks before, to be sent to Washington through channels. A look of astonishment and pleasure came over his face, followed by a feeling of supreme satisfaction as Grant took back the letter and tore it up. He had never sent it.

20

East via Chattanooga

★★★★

WHILE THE Mississippi Valley was being opened up the stalemate in Virginia continued. The eastern victory at Gettysburg was not followed up with a further offensive, and the two massive armies between Richmond and Washington resumed their postures of watchful waiting and minor skirmishing. Almost midway between Vicksburg and Gettysburg, Confederate General Bragg and Union General Rosecrans, each commanding a good-sized army, jockeyed with each other for control of eastern Tennessee. The prize was Chattanooga.

After Richmond and Vicksburg, Chattanooga was the most important strategic point in the Confederacy. Situated in the heart of a mountainous region in the southeast corner of the state, it was a gateway between the Deep South, the Southeast, and the Midwest. Railroads radiated from Chattanooga in every direction. By seizing it, the Union army would be in a position to divide the remaining half of the Confederacy by driving into Georgia in the direction of Atlanta—and then to the sea. Its control by the Rebels enabled them to shuttle reinforcements between Virginia and the South and West, and to menace Kentucky and the Ohio River Valley. The town had political as well as strategic value, for it was located in the midst of a loyal population which had been persecuted for two years for loving its country more than slavery. When, after the capture of Forts Henry and Donelson, Union gunboats steamed up the Tennessee River to that region, they found the shores lined with cheering groups of loyalists.

Bad news had come to Washington from Tennessee two months after Vicksburg's fall. General Rosecrans had maneuvered Bragg and his Rebel forces into withdrawing from Chattanooga, but then was overextended in pursuit, and two days later he was badly beaten at the battle of Chickamauga. His shattered army retreated into Chattanooga, where it was besieged, and began to suffer as badly as Pemberton had at Vicksburg. Jefferson Davis visited the Confederate camp on Lookout Mountain, one of the heights his men controlled around the city, and rejoiced that his generals had caught the Yankees "like rats in a trap."

President Lincoln and Secretary of War Stanton had one thought in the emergency. They turned to Grant. The ex-captain from Hardscrabble and Galena had become the nation's towering military leader and its sole hope for saving a key army from destruction. He alone could prevent the pendulum of war from swinging back, as it would have, if Bragg had been freed to move north and split the Union by driving through Kentucky into Ohio.

Grant received the news of the emergency at a difficult time. He was flat on his back, after a month of painful recuperation from injuries suffered during a visit to New Orleans. After his men had mopped up in Mississippi, and he had made repeated recommendations for action, which went unheeded in Washington, Grant had gone to New Orleans to confer with the commanding general there. He was reviewing troops as part of the usual military ceremony attendant upon such a visit, when the spirited horse that had been loaned to him shied at the scream of a locomotive whistle and threw his rider. Grant suffered three broken ribs, paralysis of one leg, and endured weeks of a slow and painful recovery. He was taken back to Vicksburg on a stretcher, and remained there in command of his territory while in almost constant pain. He refused to ask for a leave of absence, and from his bed had twice given orders for the shipment of troops to Tennessee to help relieve the situation there.

Without complaint or hesitation Grant answered the call from Washington to report north for further orders. He traveled to Cairo—the place from which his journey south had begun—and then to Indianapolis. There he was met by Secretary of War Stanton, who had come in person to emphasize the gravity of the crisis and to tell Grant that he was being given command of all armies west of the Allegheny Mountains. The responsibility for the forty thousand men at Chattanooga, and all they were defending, was now his.

The situation there justified the anxiety of the nation's leaders. The mountains and hills around Chattanooga to the east, south, and west formed a giant horseshoe; all were occupied by the besieging forces, who thought they had a great victory within their grasp. The Union troops were cut off from food or supplies except for one mountain trail that could not carry enough traffic to support a fraction of the number of men who were trapped there. Ten thousand horses and mules, essential to artillery and cavalry, not to mention supply trains, had already starved. Winter was closing in and the fuel within Union lines was practically exhausted.

Grant, still very lame and in pain, began at once a perilous journey. By train, on horseback through the mountains, and carried at times between two soldiers, he reached Chattanooga, "wet, dirty, and well." Immediately things began to happen.

On the very night of his arrival Grant called in and repeatedly questioned all responsible officers, to get a picture of the new theater of war that he had entered for the first time. He sat in front of a blazing fire with the floor around him wet from the water trickling from his travel-stained clothes, listened silently, and studied the maps that were placed before him. Then he turned to a desk and began to write out orders in his usual cool and businesslike way.

One of Grant's greatest talents was an ability to keep the vast and complex problems of a military region in his mind and to issue the necessary orders to each of a great number of subordinate officers within a short space of time in dispatches that were clear, distinct, and written with an economy of language. But he was not an armchair general. He insisted on spending time each day in visiting outposts and inspecting terrain, so that the orders he gave were meaningful. An officer superintending a work party, laying a pontoon bridge late at night, would hear a patter of hoofs in the darkness. A mounted man with a graying beard would ride up, ask a few questions without "pulling rank," and then ride off. But the men and their officer would recognize Grant, and such visits at one in the morning would raise their spirits tremendously, and those of all who would hear of the incident.

The first move needed at Chattanooga was to open up a supply line. The ingenious plan by which this was done, making use of two river crossings to get to a road that shortened by many miles the trip to the nearest rail line, was not invented by Grant, but to him must go the credit for recognizing the merit of the plan and giving the orders to put it into effect.

After the supply line was opened up and secured, there remained the greater task of rehabilitating the besieged army, securing reinforcements, and strengthening its outposts in preparation for an attack to break out and destroy or disperse the besieging army. Reinforcements came from the east, in a miracle of rail transportation that was devised by the President and Secretary of War, and from the west—Grant's own Vicksburg veterans, now under the command of Sherman. Center and guiding force of all the preparation was Grant himself. His function in the development of the battle of Chattanooga has been justly compared to that of a quietly spinning dynamo in a powerhouse, transmitting the current that effectively turned a whole system of wheels, most of which had laboriously ground to a halt before his arrival.

One day during an inspection trip Grant, with a bugler as companion, rode down to a point on Chattanooga Creek, which enters the Tennessee River near Lookout Mountain, one of the neighboring heights dominated by the besieging forces. When the pair rode near to one camp of pickets, he heard the corporal give the order, "Turn out the guard for the commanding general." He called out in reply, "Never mind the guard!" and his men went back to their tents. Nearby, just across the creek and within earshot, was a group of Confederate pickets. The sentinel on duty there barked out the order, "Turn out the guard for the commanding general, General Grant." The line of battle-worn Rebels front-faced to the north and gave a salute which Grant returned.

As he thought about these and the other men who fought him at Chattanooga, Grant reflected later,

> There was no time during the rebellion when I did not think, and often say, that the South was even more to be benefited by its defeat than the North. They were burdened by an institution abhorrent to all civilized people not brought up under it, and one which degraded labor, kept it in ignorance, and wore out its governing class. The labor of the country was not skilled, nor allowed to become so. The whites could not toil without becoming degraded, and those who did were contemptuously called "poor white trash." The system of labor would soon have exhausted the soil and left the people poor.

The battle for Chattanooga began like a great Greek tragedy staged in a huge amphitheater. The battlefield was much like a horseshoe-shaped football stadium, with the Confederates in the bleachers and the national forces fighting their way up from the field. The city was girded by two major hills, Lookout Mountain on one side and Missionary Ridge on the other, both occupied by the enemy.

Grant's plan was to develop pressure all along the line and then to concentrate an attack at one end of the ridge. When this gained ground, and then slowed up, the brunt of the battle was shifted to another point, further down the ridge, by the core of the army that had been defeated at Chickamauga and then besieged. The men received orders to take the first row of Confederate trenches. In one of the most dramatic acts of insubordination in the history of infantry warfare, the men, after gaining their objective, went on and on up the ridge to the second and third lines, driving all before them. Wave upon wave of the battle-hardened veterans went up to the top, and the besieging army broke and fled.

The following day was Thanksgiving, 1863. The completeness of the victory was hailed across the nation. It was the most stunning of the war.

21

To Washington—and into Virginia

★★★★

ON MARCH 8, 1864, the afternoon train to Washington arrived with its typical quota of passengers from the North and West—politicians, war contractors, lawyers, officers and men returning from leave. There was the usual rush of the out-of-towners to the Willard Hotel to register for rooms. A short, round-shouldered man in a seedy-looking general's uniform waited his turn in line, holding a briefcase in one hand and the hand of a fourteen-year-old boy with the other. The desk clerk, with instinctive disdain for the insignificant, hardly looked down at the register, and assigned the pair to a fifth-floor walkup room.

When the new guests started across the lobby to the stairs, the clerk saw a bustle and a hubbub begin around them and looked down again to read on the open page: "U. S. Grant and son, Galena, Ill." Quickly transforming himself into an attitude of proper deference, the clerk breathlessly ran over to Fred and his father and explained that there had been a mistake, that the best rooms on the second floor had been reserved for them by the War Department. He had expected the star guest to arrive with a whole retinue of aides and attendants. The visit to Washington was in response to a summons from the Administration: Grant was about to be received at the White House to be commissioned personally by President Lincoln as the first

Lieutenant General with permanent rank since Washington, and to be given command of all the Armies of the United States.

A new and, as it turned out, the final phase of the Civil War was about to begin. Despite Grant's successes in the Mississippi Valley and Tennessee, and the increasingly effective work of the Union navy's blockade, the Confederate forces in the East had kept intact the lines of defense of the vast southeastern area. The remaining Rebel territory, though war-worn, was still full of fight. Their press had concealed the extent of their losses; their war aims were to defend what remained of their territory until the divided North, harassed by slavery's sympathizers within, should press for peace at any price. The 1864 elections were looked to as the source of hope for this change. The situation in northern Virginia told the story. There had been a series of advances and retreats, over a three year period, without substantial gain to either side, at the price of a quarter of a million casualties to both sides.

Lincoln had come to realize that the source of his difficulty was the absence of unified command. His problem, until the beginning of 1864, had been that he had found no one whom he could trust. He and the nation had made the decision that had almost been inevitable after the battle of Chattanooga: to call in from the West the still shy and reticent man, whose genius was obscured by his personality, and whose determination, loyal and single-minded, was as great as his military ability.

On the evening of his arrival in Washington, Grant went to the White House to meet the President for the first time. He had been told that there would be a reception and expected others to be there, but did not know there would be such a motley crowd; the richly dressed, the uniformed, and the sightseers and self-seekers—all mingled together in a multitude that frightened him. He was wondering how to get away when the President called out to him and took his right hand warmly in both of his own. The meeting was as dramatic as it was historic—the tall, gaunt, sad-eyed Lincoln facing the modest, almost timid, ordinary-looking General. Secretary of State Seward made Grant's embarrassment complete by making him stand on a sofa so that all could see him.

Before Grant left the White House, Lincoln drew him aside for a private word. "When I present your commission to you," he whispered, "I'll say a few words, not a speech but a sentence or two." He pretended to ignore the uncomfortable glance Grant gave him. "I'll give you a copy of what I'm going to say, and you might have an answer ready." Sensing what Grant was thinking, he added, "I'll read mine." Grant thought to himself, "Then I can read mine too, and write it out in advance."

As he left the White House he said to a friend accompanying him, "I hope to get away from Washington as soon as possible, for I am tired of the show business already." He felt better when he got back to his hotel and found that Julia and Rawlins had arrived and were waiting with Fred to hear of how Lincoln and the crowd at the reception had greeted him.

After the "show business" the next day, the President and the new commanding general had a private talk. Lincoln told Grant that he had never professed to be a military man or to know how campaigns should be conducted. He had never wanted to interfere, and yet procrastination on the part of previous commanders, and pressure from the people at the North, and from Congress, had repeatedly forced him to issue "orders" which might have been all wrong—but at a time when lack of action would have been worse.

"All I want," said the President, "is someone to take the responsibility and *act,* and call upon me for all the assistance he needs. I pledge you that I shall use all the power of government in giving such assistance."

"Mr. President," answered Grant, "I will do the best I can

with the means at hand, and avoid as far as possible annoying you or the War Department."

Lincoln soon found that the faith he had placed in this man he had never met before was to be justified. Within a few months after Grant took over supreme command, the President confided in a friend: "Grant is the first General I ever had. You know how it has been with all the rest. As soon as I put a man in command of the Army, he'd come to me with a plan of campaign and about as much as say, 'Now, I don't believe I can do it, but if you say so, I'll try it on,' and so put the responsibility of success or failure on me. They all wanted me to be the General. Now, it isn't so with Grant. He hasn't told what his plans are. I don't know and I don't want to know. I am glad to find a man that can go ahead without me. When any of the rest set out on a campaign, they would look over matters and pick out some one thing they were short of and they knew I couldn't give 'em and tell me that they couldn't hope to win unless they had it."

Grant returned to the West, to meet and confer with Sherman, who was to take over his former command in the valley of the Mississippi. To Sherman he entrusted the plan of campaign that he had himself worked out and prepared during the winter for the armies of the West. They were to strike out from Chattanooga, in the direction of Atlanta, and from there to the sea. There was now to be one important difference. Sherman's campaign was to be part of Grant's over-all strategy to win the war, namely, to destroy the great armies that Lee commanded in northern Virginia.

Until Grant's assumption of command, Union forces had been acting independently, like a "balky team of horses," he said, no two pulling together. As a result, the struggle had been prolonged, the expenditure of human life greater, and the cost multiplied. The uncoordinated armies and sometimes almost inconsistent campaigns had produced confusion and uncertainty in the field and doubt, dejection and sometimes despondency at home.

BETTMANN ARCHIVE

Ulysses S. Grant receives his commission as Lieutenant-General from President Lincoln on March 9, 1864.

Grant saw clearly the nature of the problem that he faced. It was a military as well as a political problem. In the first place, from the purely military point of view the Southern armies had to be beaten. This could only be done by a breakthrough on one of the major fronts or by such constant pressure on all fronts that the Rebel armies would fall apart from exhaustion and depletion. The campaign that he was about to launch was the culmination of what he had achieved by the successes in the West: the creation of a "rear" in the Confederacy that at the beginning of the war had had no rear.

The political side of the 1864 military campaign was grasped instinctively and thoroughly by a commanding general who had no background at all as a politician, and who believed devotedly in the subordination of the military commander to the civilian government. It was as a part of his very generalship that he saw how political changes could hamper or defeat the Army in the accomplishment of its mission. Disgruntled, proslavery General McClellan, removed from command for ineffectiveness in the early Virginia battles, was running for President against Lincoln on a platform calling for peace with slavery. Grant recognized that the re-election of Lincoln would be a greater triumph over the principles of the rebellion than any military victory could have been. At the same time, by the very character of his conduct of the war, he made that re-election possible.

22

Victory

★★★★

EARLY IN MAY, when the South was filled with the fragrance of its blossoms, and men should have been planting, ploughing, and putting cattle out to pasture, the signal was flashed by Grant for every general to move forward. The big push at the beginning was that of the Army of the Potomac, the battle-hardened veterans whose comrades had died in Virginia, Maryland, and Pennsylvania, and who had never been outfought but only out-generaled. At the same time as Grant moved across the Rapidan River in northern Virginia, Sherman began the long march across the heart of the South through the Chattanooga gateway.

Reorganized and re-equipped, the masses of men moved forward. The first of what were to be a dozen bloody battles was fought in a tangled, wooded, primitive area known as the Wilderness, where movements at midday were almost as obscured as they would have been at night. The forces under Lee were more familiar with the ground they were fighting defensively, and had been rallied to the struggle with the knowledge that only by a supreme effort could their cause be saved.

Grant was faced with a new test of his qualities as a leader, a test of nerve and will such as few had ever faced. Lee's generalship and his men's fury created crises before which anyone but Ulysses Grant would have flinched. The death toll in the Wilderness must have brought home to him what no planning could have anticipated:

the tragic implications of what had to be done. Defeat often seemed close, and disaster might threaten, but his grim determination was not affected. When the battle was at its worst, he sat smoking a pipe, his face in repose. He must have known the extent of the danger and yet gave orders calmly, without a sign of tension. At one point an orderly rushed up and shouted, "They have broken through! Hancock has given way."

"I don't believe it," he answered. He told the man, "You must be tired and nervous, go in and rest for a while."

He did not flinch when over the roar of cannon he would hear the fierce, peculiar battle-shriek of five thousand charging Rebels. At one point a shell struck quite near him and furrowed a path in the ground before exploding. Grant neither jumped nor ran, but pulled a small compass from his pocket to detect the course of the shell, and then sent out orders to his artillery commander.

To those who did not know Grant, it seemed as if he never thought of the dying or the dead. Rawlins was the only man in Grant's tent the evening he received the most appalling casualty list, and saw him walk back inside, after giving his final orders for the day, and throw himself downward on to the cot and sob. "He was cruel only to be kind," said Rawlins. The war was on; it was none of his doing: it had to be brought to an end; 130,000 had died in the East, without result, and a prolonged war or a truce on slavery's terms would only lead to greater losses.

The battle of the Wilderness in which such bloody losses were sustained has been called a draw by superficial critics. It was so in the sense that no obvious tactical or strategic gain was made, and yet Grant's initial purpose was achieved. He had come to grips with Lee's well-advertised army and had begun the process of wearing it down. He had put himself in position to prevent Lee from reinforcing the other great Rebel army that was facing Sherman before Atlanta. His program for restoring peace was in action.

After two days in the Wilderness, Grant gave orders to his men to withdraw from their positions. There was nothing further to be achieved in that arena. The men awaited new orders as they marched, mindful of the many occasions on which past generals had clashed with Lee or Jackson and then withdrawn. At a certain point in the road if they had turned to the left, it would have meant retreat. They turned to the right. "Instantly all of us heard a sigh of relief," one private wrote in his diary. "Our spirits rose. We marched free. The men began to sing. The enlisted men understood the flanking movement. That night we were happy."

As Grant rode down the pike with his aides, soldiers weary and sleepy after long battles sprang to their feet and swarmed to the roadside. Men waved their hats and pressed forward to the roadside, clapping their hands. The assurance of continued advance, after the years of indecision and retreat, inspired the new armies under his command with a trust in their chief which could not afterwards be shaken. Three days later, after further fearful fights, Grant electrified the nation with a dispatch to Washington reporting the heavy losses on both sides and concluding: "I propose to fight it out on this line if it takes all summer."

It was to take more than the summer. There was one great opportunity planned by Grant and lost by the ineptitude of his subordinate generals. If they had not failed their chief, the breakthrough would have come and the war would have been won by the bravery and determination of Negro soldiers at the battle of Petersburg.

In reorganizing the Armies of the Potomac and James, Grant had ordered that twenty thousand Negro troops, infantry and cavalry, be transferred east from the Mississippi and Tennessee fronts, where he had first learned of their worth. In mid-June Grant ordered an attack on Petersburg, a town twenty miles south of Richmond, to be made by forces from the Army of the James. Petersburg was a key railroad and communications center, through which passed most of the supplies that Richmond and Lee's armies needed. It was strongly fortified but for the time being only lightly manned. The battle plan called for an attack by other troops on Petersburg while Grant's armies were moving further into Virginia, across the James River, to attack Lee and Richmond from the southwest.

Shortly after daybreak on June 15 troops under General W. F. Smith, including four regiments of Negroes, advanced to the attack. Through swampy woods the Negro troops advanced and took a key outpost under murderous shellfire, after a charge up a slope. Their next assignment was the main lines of Confederate fortifications. When the orders came for a further charge, the Negro soldiers advanced successfully again and seized the portion of the main fortifications that had been their objective. One black regiment lost 250 out of 600 men in the attack. After the Rebels withdrew, General Smith appeared at the camp of the Negro volunteers and told them he was proud of their courage and spirit. They had no superiors as soldiers, he said, and repeated this praise in his reports to the War Department.

Despite this initial success, Petersburg was not then taken. A delay by Smith in following up the first day's fighting gave Lee an opportunity to pour reinforcements into the town, which had become the key to the advance on Richmond. There followed a long-drawn-out siege that was destined to last until the eve of the collapse of the Confederacy.

While Grant was keeping Lee engaged before Petersburg, and steadily wearing down his main body of troops, the spectacular military victories essential to ultimate success were being won elsewhere. General Philip Sheridan, whom Grant had chosen to command the Union cavalry and given orders to fight as an independent force, won victory after victory in the Shenandoah Valley of Virginia during the summer and early autumn. On September 2, while McClellan was being formally nominated to oppose Lincoln for the Pres-

BETTMANN ARCHIVE

Grant moves his armies further into Virginia, across the James River, to attack Richmond from the southwest.

idency, by a convention that was denouncing the war as a failure, General Sherman was entering the key city of Atlanta. These victories made possible the political gains in the 1864 election that Grant had seen as essential to the final victory.

Sherman's advances continued through the winter, as Grant carried on the stubborn, long and hard siege of Petersburg. The Southern people grew weary and disenchanted with the war into which they had been led. The Confederate armies, who had fought bravely, began to lose by desertions as many as they did from casualties on the field. As spring approached in 1865 it became possible for the armies of Virginia to move and maneuver. An attack was made which threatened the encirclement of Petersburg, and Richmond fell soon afterwards. Lee's armies began their final retreat.

23

"The Rebels Are Our Countrymen Again"

★★★★

NEVER IN THE history of the world had there been as great or as costly a rebellion as the American Civil War. It was, moreover, the first modern or "total" war. It was shocking in its casualty lists and unprecedented in the devastation that had to be inflicted on the South to destroy its will to fight. Ulysses Grant never forgot for a moment, however, that the enemy he was relentlessly pursuing and destroying had been his neighbors and kinsmen yesterday and would be tomorrow.

While chasing the still considerable remnants of Lee's army after the fall of Richmond, Grant met a Virginian who was an officer in his army, and who had come from a dramatic confrontation with a cousin, Confederate General Ewell, just captured by the Union forces. This officer reported to Grant that the Rebel officer corps knew that their cause was lost and had felt it was the duty of the group of men who called themselves the Confederate Government to make peace—but the latter balked. "He told me," said Smith, "that for every man killed after this in the war, somebody was responsible, and it would be but very little better than murder."

Grant did not wait long on hearing this or stand on ceremony. He wrote Lee, asking the surrender of his army. There was need for diplomacy. Lee would not admit his case was hopeless, yet knew it was, and was tempted to inquire as to Grant's terms. Grant, knowing that the great object now was to draw Lee into a capitulation and avoid the lengthy and bloody guerrilla warfare that Jefferson Davis seemed to want, said that there was but one condition: that Lee's men pledge not to take up arms again. Lee hesitated at first, but Grant's simple directness—and the seizure of three trains of supplies by Union cavalry—persuaded him to agree to a meeting.

At the house of a man named McClean in the little Virginia village of Appomattox Courthouse occurred the most dramatic of all the military meetings of our history. Two generals who had come to be symbols of their armies and of the different societies they represented faced each other: the democrat Grant and the aristocrat Lee.

"What General Lee's feelings were, I do not know," said Grant later. "They were entirely concealed from my observation; but my own feelings, which had been quite jubilant on the receipt of his letter, were sad and depressed. I felt like anything rather than rejoicing at the downfall of a foe who had fought so long and valiantly and had suffered so much for a cause, though that cause was, I believe, one of the worst for which a people ever fought and one for which there was the least excuse."

Grant talked for a while of ordinary things, hesitating to come to the point or force the conversation on to it. They exchanged small talk about old Army days, service in Mexico, and so on, until Lee reminded Grant that they had business to do and asked what were the terms that Grant proposed to give his army. Grant told him that the principal point he had in mind was that the men lay down their arms, give their word they would not return to the fight—and that was all. After another exchange of small talk, Lee suggested that the terms be written out.

A table was brought over and Grant wrote, swiftly and clearly as usual, although he did not know when he sat down what the first words would be. The key phrase that came to his mind expressed the most that he, as military commander, could do to insure that when the war ended there would be no vindictive policy toward the vanquished soldiers: "Each officer and man will be allowed to return to his home, not to be disturbed by United States authority so long as they observe their paroles and the laws in force where they reside."

As he wrote, another thought came to him. He had come, on short notice, battle-stained, in a private's blouse on which were sewn the marks of his rank—but with no sword. Lee had dressed himself with care for the ceremony, immaculately, in a spotless gray uniform emphasizing his haughty bearing; he wore embroidered gauntlets and a dress sword of the sort likely to have been presented to him by admirers. There flashed into Grant's mind the thought of sparing the conquered foe the humiliation of surrendering such insignia. Then it was that he wrote another line permitting officers to retain their sidearms, horses, and personal effects.

When the written terms were handed to Lee and he read them over and came to this sentence—which had not previously been discussed—he looked up and remarked with more feeling than he had shown through the entire interview, "This will have a happy effect on my army."

He paused a moment and then asked about the enlisted men in the artillery and cavalry. Unlike the Union army, he explained, most of them owned their own horses, and he requested that they be permitted to retain them. Grant realized the situation. Most of the men in the ranks were small farmers. The bulk of the Southern countryside had been raided by the two armies so much so that he doubted whether they would be able to put in a crop to carry themselves and their families through the next winter without the aid of the horses they were then riding.

"The United States does not want those farmers' horses, General," he declared. "I shall instruct the officers who are to receive the parole of your men to let every man of the Confederate army who claims to own a horse or mule to take it home."

Thus, in all that he did during the meeting, Grant the soldier was conscious of the hard, unhappy years that were to face the nation of civilians who had suffered such a bloody and costly division. He knew that to heal it required a heroic quality on each side, and he was determined to make his own contribution and take the first step without, however, interfering with the supremacy of the central government. The tragedy of the period that followed was that Grant's instinctively noble efforts were thwarted by a series of events that began with the assassination of President Lincoln.

But at Appomattox, Grant triumphed. He achieved, with a touch of genius, just what he had set out to do—although, like his approach to a problem arising in the heat of battle, he may not have known precisely when he started what he was going to do.

As he left the McClean homestead that day he heard one of his officers give orders for a hundred-gun salute, the natural military reaction to the great triumph that all were to celebrate. "No, men," he said, "no cannonade. The Rebels are our countrymen again."

The next day he rode out beyond the Union lines toward Lee's headquarters, and Lee, seeing who it was, came to meet him. Lee assured Grant of the great and favorable impression the terms of surrender had made on the men in gray, and promised that the entire South would respond to the generosity he had displayed. Scores of the captured officers had already visited Grant, many of them schoolmates from West Point or comrades from the Mexican War, and they thanked him for their swords, their liberty, and the practical immunity from civil prosecution he had granted them by the phrase "not to be disturbed by United States authority."

Grant and Lee talked about the need for peace. Lee hoped that there would be no further sacrifice of life but was cautious; the South was a large area, and some time might pass before men laid down their arms everywhere. Grant responded by saying that Lee's influence was greater than any other man in the Confederacy, and urged him to advise the surrender of the other armies. This Lee would not do without consulting President Jefferson Davis. To save the lives of his own half-starving men, he took upon himself the authority to surrender them; further than that he would not go and Grant knew it would be useless to insist.

Grant saluted and went back to his headquarters to prepare for a trip to Washington. There was much to be done to cut down on the expense of running a war that had been going full blast until the day before. On his way to Washington he looked forward to the pleasure of reporting in person to the sad-faced Commander-in-Chief, who had trusted him throughout, and whose trust had been vindicated.

24

The Nation's Loss

★★★★

"JUST A MOMENT, General," called out the President as Grant began to leave the Cabinet Room at the White House. "Mrs. Lincoln and I are going to the theater tonight, and we would be very happy to have you and Mrs. Grant join us."

"I'm afraid we can't," Grant answered regretfully. "I'm sure Mrs. Grant will be awfully sorry not to be able to go, but we are expected to go to Burlington, New Jersey, tonight, to see our three oldest children who are in school there."

"The people would be so pleased to see you," pressed the President. "You really ought to come."

Of course, for the crowd-shy soldier, if there had been any doubt about his not going to Ford's Theater on April 14, 1865—five days after Lee's surrender—the promise of audience adulation would have clinched his decision against it. It had been settled by Julia early in the day, however, that nothing except an emergency should keep them from going to the New Jersey school to see the children. She did not, of course, have to ask twice to get her husband to promise that he would come too if he could get through enough of the paper work of the first stage of the demobilization planning.

When Grant returned to their hotel room later that day, Julia told him about an evil-looking man who had seemed to be staring most intently at her and little Jesse when they had lunch in the hotel dining room. Later, as they rode to the railroad station, a horseman galloped over to their unescorted carriage as it was driving along and leaned down to peer inside.

"It's the same man," Julia cried out.

Grant signaled to stop the carriage and looked after the departing horseman. "What would he want with us?" he remarked. They thought no more about the two incidents until they reached Philadelphia. There they stopped at a hotel dining room for a late snack, while waiting for the New Jersey ferry, and while they were eating a messenger rushed over. Grant reached for the telegram which the man handed to him, looked at the message, and then lowered his head sadly. Abraham Lincoln had been shot and was dying. The deed occurred at the theater, in the very box where Julia and he might have been. A chapter in American history had ended and a new one was to begin.

When he heard the news of Lincoln's murder, one secessionist politician, Benjamin Hill of Georgia, cried out, "God help us if that is true. It is the worst blow that has yet been struck the South." Grant himself, in later years, called it the darkest day in his life. Nothing could have happened that threatened more gravely what he had begun at Appomattox, the effort to bring about the beginning of a peace based on reunion. Much as the nation had needed a Lincoln to lead it in the war for freedom and nationhood, it needed him even more badly now. Never had the country faced more difficult problems, and never did it find itself with a President less suitable than Lincoln's successor for meeting and solving them.

For four years the North and South had been arrayed against each other in bloody conflict. That one had crushed the other by force was not enough to revive a common national feeling among the divided descendants of the men who had won their independence less than nine decades before. In every state there were homes with empty seats at the table—fathers, brothers, sons, were never to return. In many places the homes themselves were no longer standing. Atrocity tales—many of them true—about treatment of prisoners of war created antagonism and mistrust. The murder of President Lincoln became the greatest atrocity of all and aroused the harshest feelings; Northern willingness to believe that Confederate leaders were behind Booth's mad act angered many at the South.

The nation that was so torn and saddened faced two great and perplexing problems—each without precedent, and each complicated by the existence of the other. What was to be done about the four million human beings who were no longer slaves—and yet who could not be free until a way of life was provided for them while they learned to adjust to the world about them? What was to be done about the disintegrated state and local governments in the seceded states, whose public officials had violated their oath of office when secession began, and who lost all claim to act when the Confederacy fell apart?

Men of compassion and understanding, without extreme convictions or partisan motivation, had thought hard and earnestly about these great problems. They saw the difficulties of the peace as requiring rarer qualities and higher talents than were needed to win a war. The nation's leaders, they reasoned, had to do more for the Negro than merely emancipate him in name. He must be given an economic base for his existence, and a right, like any other laborer, to participate in his government so that he could help protect his rights. The poor whites of the South could be forgiven for having fought for a cause the true nature of which they did not understand, and of which they were as much the victim as the slave. The seceded states must be restored to the Union, but the national Government had to be careful of the manner of their return: "Dependent provinces sullenly submitting to a destiny which they loathe would be a burden to us," wrote James Russell Lowell, who was a political analyst and editor as well as a poet. The ex-Rebel states were not at all identical in their history, outlook, or population, he pointed out, and what might do well for Tennessee might not be suitable for South Carolina.

The gentle, wise, and patient Lincoln had seen this. He had begun a policy in 1863 that was meant to help encourage loyal groups in partially liberated states to resume normal relations with Washington by the establishment of provisional governments under executive control. He offered amnesty to all Confederates (except those who had deserted United States posts in 1861, mistreated Union prisoners, or held the rank of colonel or higher in the Rebel forces) who would agree to take an oath to support the Constitution. These offers of Lincoln were wartime measures, intended to help hasten the coming of the peace; they were not necessarily intended to determine the nature of the permanent peace settlement. As with every other situation that he faced during his Presidency, Lincoln would have met the problem in the light of conditions as they might develop—not on the basis of some preconceived plan or notion.

There were, however, two fundamental elements of Lincoln's thinking that came more and more to the fore as the end of the war drew near. In the first place, he insisted on several occasions that a state could not take its rightful place back in the Union in circumstances which would turn its government over to enemies of the Union. Those who had been the leading force in seceding from and levying war against the United States would have to be excluded.

The second point on which Lincoln insisted was that amnesty and forgiveness to those who had fought against the Union must be accompanied by universal suffrage. He said he regarded it as "a religious duty" that he owed to the colored race to help to better their condition, since they "have so heroically vindicated their manhood on the battlefield, where, in assisting to save the life of the Republic, they have demonstrated in blood their right to the ballot." He went on to add with great emphasis:

"The restoration of the Rebel states to the Union must

rest on the principle of civic and political equality of both races; and it must be sealed by general amnesty."

The turmoil of the next three years, the tragedy of the next dozen, the injustice of the next hundred—all stemmed from Andrew Johnson's refusal to act upon these principles that Lincoln had stated.

The nation's calamity in Lincoln's death was a double one. It was not only in the loss of the one man who had the wisdom, the compassion, and the firmness to lead the nation to a just peace. It was also in the entry into the White House of the man who succeeded him.

25

Immediate Postwar Difficulties

★★★★

As a stranger in Washington, Grant began the difficult postwar period knowing hardly half a dozen members of Congress by name. He was in new surroundings, in the midst of unfamiliar politicians and officials, facing novel problems. As ex-captain he had rejoined the Army after an absence of seven years and had little practical experience in the relation of civilian to military officers.

Before he could plunge completely into the task of demobilization and the work of running a peacetime Army, Grant had to await the news of the final operations of the remaining field armies he commanded. The Confederacy had practically fallen apart as an organized government, and Lee had surrendered its largest single force. The most important remaining group of Rebel soldiers was commanded by General Joseph E. Johnston in North Carolina. They faced and were outnumbered by Sherman's men, who were in fighting trim after having marched through Georgia and South Carolina.

Grant confidently expected Sherman to receive Johnston's surrender on terms similar to those he had given Lee at Appomattox. However, the news that clicked in on the telegraph keys on April 21, a week after Lincoln's death, was not at all what Grant had expected. The peacetime commander was called upon to respond to an emergency which required exercise of judgment and tact rather than military skill, and which required coordination with civilian officials.

Sherman reported that he had entered into an agreement which (he said) would bring peace throughout the balance of Confederate territory, if approved by the President. The agreement he had made with Johnston had been signed, he reported, by John C. Breckenridge, Rebel "Secretary of War," and therefore it covered all Rebel forces, not merely those in North Carolina. The price that Sherman had agreed to pay for this was startling: the units of the surrendered armies were to be allowed to march in bodies to their respective state capitals; they were to deposit their arms in state arsenals; the existing, disloyal state governments were to be recognized, provided their leaders took a new oath of allegiance; all franchise and "property" rights of white Southerners would be respected and protected, and a general amnesty declared.

Grant was aghast. He knew little of politics but enough of the duties of a soldier to know that Sherman had, by far, transgressed the limitations of an officer of an army of a republic. This was no mere truce or armistice that Sherman was reporting; it was to all intents and purposes a treaty of peace. Sherman had taken it upon himself, single-handed, to settle the whole complex and grave question of restoration of the Southern states, over which Lincoln had contended with his Congress, and which President Johnson, his advisors, and leading senators and congressmen were now debating.

When he could not locate his superior, Secretary of War Edwin M. Stanton, at the War Department, Grant rushed a message to him. He reported the receipt of news from Sherman, which he described "as being of such importance that I think immediate action should be taken." He specified that it was necessary that a "meeting take place tonight" of the President and his Cabinet. Sherman had been Grant's friend and, besides Sheridan, his most loyal and efficient subordinate for the last two years of the war. With the aid of his brother, John Sherman, Senator from Ohio, he had checked an attempt to elevate him over Grant that some impetuous congressmen started when Sherman captured Atlanta while Grant seemed stalled with Lee in front of Petersburg. Sherman knew, as these men did not, that Grant's grip on Lee was essential to his own success. Grant realized that all this could not affect his duty to undo Sherman's great blunder, and he did not shrink from doing so.

All present at the late-evening Cabinet meeting that Grant initiated agreed in disapproving Sherman's terms of truce. Grant stubbornly resisted those who questioned his friend's motives and would have censured him personally. Grant saw the importance of defending the principle that generals could not meddle in politics, but would not permit Sherman's reputation to be destroyed for his error of judgment.

It was agreed after heated discussion that the President should direct Sherman to give the forty-eight hour notice of intention to resume hostilities that was required to terminate the truce. Some were insisting that this could only be done by relieving Sherman from command, when Grant asked to be heard.

"You cannot remove him from command of the army he has just led to victory," he insisted. "Let me go down and take charge of straightening this out myself."

"The man's a traitor or a fool," answered Secretary of War Stanton.

"He's neither," responded Grant. "He's entitled to make a mistake like this once, and it is not irreparable. His terms did provide that they would have to be reviewed by the President, and so he left us free to reject them. Sherman has done too much for his country to be removed or even censured. I request that I be allowed to take the news of your disapproval to him myself."

In this immediate postwar period Grant's popularity and prestige was greater than anyone except George Washington himself had ever attained. It was not easy to deny such a request when he made it.

His friend's wisdom and tact helped tremendously in making it possible for Sherman to correct his error without undue humiliation. Grant quietly slipped down to Sherman's field headquarters in Raleigh, North Carolina, and would not let it be known that he was there except to the necessary few on the commander's staff. He quietly explained to Sherman what had to be done and then left as quietly and as inconspicuously as he had come. As a result, the revocation of the improvident truce seemed to be Sherman's own decision, taken on his own responsibility.

Grant's quick intervention in that matter had helped sustain the supremacy of civilian authority. He also knew when to stand fast in resisting the encroachment of civilian interference with military decisions.

One day, a few weeks after his return from North Carolina, he was relaxing with Rawlins at a game of billiards in a Washington hotel. An army major entered and whispered to him. Grant lay down his cue at once and said, "Rawlins, don't disturb the balls until I come back."

He ran out of the hotel and into the street. There he found a mounted sentinel, and he motioned to the private to give him the horse. Grant jumped into the saddle and galloped up Pennsylvania Avenue to the War Department. There he asked at once to be admitted to the office of the Secretary of War.

"Mr. Secretary," he said, after exchanging greetings, "I am given to understand that you have issued orders for the arrest of General Lee."

"I have issued orders for the arrest of a number of prominent Confederates," answered Stanton.

"Mr. Secretary," said Grant firmly, after a moment's pause, "when General Lee surrendered to me, I gave him my word and honor that none of his army, nor himself, would be disturbed, as long as they kept their parole. I must ask that those arrests be canceled."

Stanton referred Grant to the President. The General hurried to the White House, where he spoke bluntly.

"A general commanding troops has certain responsibilities and duties which are supreme," he said. "I made certain terms with Lee, the best and only terms. If I had told him that his liberty or that of his officers or men, could be touched, or that they could be disturbed by civil authority, Lee would not have surrendered, and we would have lost many lives."

"They have been accused of treason by a Grand Jury at Norfolk," interrupted the President. "Arson is a crime, and murder is a crime, and treason is a crime, and crime must be punished."

Grant flushed, but answered quickly. "I will resign the command of the army rather than execute any order directing me to arrest Lee or any of his commanders so long as they keep their parole and obey the laws."

Grant's resignation and resulting popular protest was a possibility which the President did not dare to face.

"When can these men be tried?" asked Johnson.

"Never, Mr. President, unless they violate their paroles," answered Grant.

President Johnson's vindictive expressions were to continue for some months, and it was only Grant's firmness that protected the good faith of the Government and prevented the arrest of many Confederate officers. In consequence, there grew up toward Grant a warm feeling throughout the South. At the beginning of this postwar period he reciprocated that feeling. He wrote to Julia from Sherman's headquarters on that first postwar trip to North Carolina: "The suffering that must exist in the South next year, even with the war ending now, will be beyond conception." He deplored "people who talk of further retaliation and punishment," and ended his letter, as always, "Love and kisses to you and the children."

26

The Greatest Problem of the Peace

★★★★

THE WORD "reconstruct" has two dictionary definitions. It means either to "rebuild" or to "make over." There was much that had to be rebuilt in the region that had just surrendered. The local governments had fallen apart with defeat and their political relations with the central Government had been disrupted. Most of their railroads and many of their homes and factory or warehouse buildings had been damaged or destroyed, some by advancing and some by retreating armies. The principal economic activity, agriculture, had been halted in most areas with the outlawing of slavery. There was little that did not have to be either rebuilt or made over.

If there had been substantial sentiment in the South in 1865 that supported the idea that the Negro was a free human being, entitled to all that freedom implies, and southern leaders had decided to promote this feeling, our history would have been quite different. It would have been seen that genuine freedom requires, in an agricultural area, an opportunity to work one's own land and to secure an education. The nation's new candidates for citizenship would have been guided in their work and development toward full freedom. Those hundreds of thousands of Negroes who were already free before the war and of whom many were more educated than the mass of poor whites, and Negroes who had joined the Union army and learned to read with a musket in one hand and a speller in the other—all would have been granted the right to vote as a matter of course, as Grant had urged in his talks with Chaplain Eaton three years before. The rest would have been entitled to receive the right to vote at least as quickly as the immigrant European peasantry that had come from famine-ridden countries and wretched hovels that were hardly better than the slave quarters of the South. There should have developed a partnership between the peoples of the South, in which the most talented and creative of each race would have made their contributions to the growth and enrichment of their region and their country. That this did not work out this way was the nation's greatest tragedy, a tragedy greater than the war itself, since we still suffer its consequences today.

The Reconstruction period that followed the Civil War was a failure because the South did not move under enlightened white leadership in the direction of a biracial partnership. The white leaders who tried to make a sensible and moderate beginning of a readjustment of race relationships were threatened with or suffered violence. They were driven out of public life and even out of the region. Whatever chance there had been to reconstruct the South and "make over" its race relations, as Lincoln had hoped to do, was lost during the Presidency of Andrew Johnson.

Johnson is an outstanding example of the unfortunate consequences that may follow when a man is given a nomination as vice-president to "balance" and strengthen a ticket, regardless of his lack of ability to be a national political leader. He came from Tennessee, where he was unusual in that he had risen in politics without having been a member of one of the great slaveholding families that for the most part had dominated the South and produced its prewar statesmen. Johnson remained loyal to the Union and opposed secession; when enough of his state was liberated to justify it, he was sent back to his home state to act as military governor. He was given the vice-presidential nomination in 1864 because Lincoln feared that his own chances for re-election were threatened by the campaign of General McClellan, nominated by the Democrats on a peace-with-appeasement platform. Since Johnson had been a lifelong Democrat, it was believed that his candidacy would help rally members of his party in the Northern states to support the Lincoln ticket.

Unfortunately Andrew Johnson as President was to prove himself to be an arrogant man, narrow and obstinate. He had been raised with the racial prejudices that were especially strong among those known as "poor whites." Prior to his accession to the Presidency he had hardly ever been north of the Mason-Dixon line. He knew little about Northern or Western men or their opinions. He was unfamiliar with large cities and had no firsthand knowledge of the developing industrial communities of the nation, the growth of which had been hastened by the war. He had little understanding and less sympathy for the abolitionist sentiment that had grown throughout the nation as the meaning of the war became clear. He did not share the opinion, which the Negro soldier had won, though grudgingly, from most Union veterans, that Negroes were indeed human beings entitled to equal protection of the laws.

Johnson was a partisan politician with unduly strict views about the Constitution. He was because of his outlook and character temperamentally incapable of cooperating or compromising with great congressional leaders who had come to the fore during the war years. Lincoln had been able to work with the Congress even when some of the leaders opposed particular policies. It was possible for them to meet halfway. This was never so with Johnson. Until March, 1867, he was to have the very Congress that was elected with Lincoln and himself, yet he could not work with them.

Grant, as a soldier, had always accepted the West Point tradition that the military man must stay out of politics. He did not begin his peacetime role as army commander with any particular notion about reconstruction methods. He did appreciate the value and importance of the Negro soldiers in his armies and felt an obligation to them when they returned to civilian life in their homes in the South. He also remembered the many occasions when his soldiers had been guided in strange terrain by friendly Negroes and how often, when he would lead the United States Army, under the American flag, into Southern cities, he had received a friendly reception from Negroes lining the streets, while the white population viewed them with resentment.

Grant had shown his inclination to extend compassionate and merciful treatment to the white men of the South at Appomattox, later when Lee and others were threatened with arrest, and at other times. He sincerely felt that those who had been his enemies until April, 1865, were his countrymen again. This did not mean that as former combat commander and present military administrator he was required to remain indifferent to mistreatment of his veterans and his troops in the area under military occupation. His obligation to stay out of politics did not mean that he could not react to the reports that began to come in through Army channels of atrocities being inflicted on ex-slaves who included his ex-soldiers.

Johnson, the politician, had expressed violent hostility at first to the leaders of the former Confederacy. They were the great landholding aristocrats of the South of whom, as a "poor white," he had been jealous, and he held them responsible for the tragic destiny of the South. The words "treason is a crime and crime must be punished" came readily and often to his lips.

The country feared during the first months of his Administration that the new President would be too vindictive toward his fellow Southerners. Then there began a gradual transformation. The White House began to be swamped with visitors from the aristocratic families that Johnson had previously feared and hated. Flattered by their attentions, he recognized them as political allies with a similar point of view, now that secession was out of the question. The point of view that they had in common was a belief that the Negro was lazy and shiftless; that he would not work without compulsion; and that some form of discipline as a substitute for slavery was needed to enable the South to prosper. Once imbued with this point of view, shared by some of his Northern advisers, Johnson was unable to take advantage of the great opportunity that the war's end presented to "make over" the South.

The President approached the problem of "reconstruction" as if it were a question of bringing about, as quickly as possible, political relations between the rebellious states and the Union. His intent was, without the advice or consent of Congress, to bring new state governments into being and to recognize them without imposing any conditions as to protection of the freedmen, the Union veterans, or the loyal Southerners who had risked all and lost much during the war. He rejected the idea of universal or even equal suffrage and was willing, in the final analysis, to turn the ex-Rebel states back into the hands of the men who had led them into war and secession. It was they, he thought, who could best solve the pressing economic and social problems that were the aftermath of the war.

This approach troubled the national political leaders in Congress and the loyal states, particularly those who saw the Negro as entitled to full citizenship. Some accepted Johnson's policy with skepticism and a wait-and-see attitude. Others were shocked and began to speak out against it. They were powerless, for the time being, as Congress could not call itself into session and was not scheduled to meet until December.

As these events were taking shape during the summer

and autumn months of 1865, Grant was away from Washington for a good deal of the time. It became quite evident soon after Lincoln's tragic death that Grant was by far the most popular man in the country. Newspapers continually praised his achievements as a soldier; his natural modesty and quiet simplicity made him an ideal subject for hero worshipers. He was ready for a long, hard-earned vacation, and the many invitations from cities of the North suggested a pleasant way of spending his vacation for one whose boyhood love of travel remained.

With Julia and the children he spent much of the time in visits across the country, from Boston to Galena. Parades, banquets, and gala receptions were a daily occurrence. If Julia and Ulysses went to the theater, the audience would spontaneously rise to its feet and applaud for many minutes. Sometimes their carriage could hardly make its way through the streets. Gifts were heaped on him, ranging from boxes of cigars to fully furnished houses. When they arrived in Galena, a banner strung across the street announced: "General. The sidewalk is built!" This was in recollection of a half-humorous remark he had made, during his rise to fame, to the effect that after the war he would like to be mayor of Galena long enough to see to it that a sidewalk was built from the railway station to his home. He had remembered well the months during which he had had to trudge through mud or dust on his way home from the store.

27

Grant Sees Congress Break with Johnson

★★★★

GRANT HAD NOT been asked for his opinion about the wisdom of the President's rapid-reconstruction program. However, since the Congress was not in session when Johnson took office, and was not scheduled to meet for many months, it was his duty to accept and to try to live with the Johnson program. As a citizen Grant agreed with Lincoln that Congress should have the last word on the question of the restoration of the state governments in the South. As one who had said at the moment of Lee's surrender, "the Rebels are our countrymen again," he was willing to stand by and observe the experiments with a policy based on the idea of allowing the South to attempt to rehabilitate itself without outside interference.

It soon appeared that Johnson had ambitions for a second term as President and was seeking to be renominated by a new coalition of restored ex-slaveholders in the South and McClellan followers in the North, rather than by the group that brought about the renomination and re-election of Lincoln. As a shrewd politician he was conscious of Grant's immense popularity and sought to use it for his own advantage. He went out of his way to be seen with Grant, sent him notes and messages almost daily, dropped in at Army headquarters for "advice," and even appeared, unannounced and uninvited, at their home when he heard that Julia was giving a party. As the end of 1865 drew near it occurred to him to attempt to exploit Grant's prestige for his own purposes by sending him for a quick inspection tour of the South, through which he hoped to counteract the reports that were appearing in Northern newspapers and creating a state of alarm over the suspicion that the white South, after losing the war, was winning the peace. Congress was about to meet for the first time since before Lincoln's death and the effect of these reports was to mobilize sentiment in favor of rejecting Johnson's reconstruction program and substituting a plan that would provide guarantees against control by disloyal elements in the ex-Rebel states and that would forbid the mistreatment of the freedmen.

Grant, as a dutiful soldier, undertook the trip even though the time alloted hardly permitted him to see actual conditions for himself. His report states that he hurried through Virginia without talking to anyone; that he spent only one day in Raleigh, North Carolina; two days in Charleston, South Carolina; and one day each in Savannah and Augusta. Even so, he saw and heard enough to impel him to stress that no one in those states "thought it practicable to withdraw the military from the South at present, the white and black mutually requiring the protection of the General Government." He also declared that "in some form the Freedmen's Bureau is an absolute necessity until civil law is established and enforced, securing to the freedmen their rights and full protection."

This Freedmen's Bureau was a Federal agency operating under the supervision of Grant and the War Department. It was a national version of the organization that Grant had devised in Mississippi in the autumn of 1862, with Chaplain Eaton at its head, to help organize the new economic and social adjustment of the self-emancipated slaves who had swarmed to the camps of the Army of the Tennessee even before the victory at Vicksburg. In its postwar form the bureau, established by a law that had been passed while Lincoln was President, was to bring together and centralize the existing organizations for the social, economic, and legal protection of the liberated slaves.

In a third recommendation contained in his report Grant concluded with perception that "it cannot be expected that the opinions held by men in the South for years can be changed in a day, and therefore the freedmen require, for a few years, not only laws to protect them, but the fostering care of those who will give them good counsel and on whom they can rely."

Johnson disregarded these portions of Grant's report on conditions in the South, and saw to it that the Administration-influenced newspapers played up for his own propaganda purposes a sentence in which Grant said "the mass of thinking men of the South accept the present situation in good faith." Very likely the so-called thinking men who called on the general in his hotels in the places where he stopped were anxious to impress him with their loyalty and put things in a favorable light so as to insure restoration of the remaining governmental functions in their states. The basic conclusions of Grant's report, however, which Johnson was to ignore, agreed with a more detailed and impressive survey made by former General Carl Schurz, later to be a United States senator, who declared that the power of the state governments that Johnson had established without the approval of Congress was being used to reduce the freedom of the Negroes to a minimum. He also observed at first hand the beginnings of the wanton, savage outrages that were being perpetrated on unoffending Negro families.

Northern congressional leaders had become increasingly concerned over the information that they had received and its confirmation in the Grant report as well as documentation in the Schurz report. The last straw for many Americans and their representatives in Washington was news of the passage of state laws called the "Black Codes." These products of the new all-white state legislatures, who had been elected by all-white ballots, seemed to most observers to be an attempt to restore slavery in all but name. They varied from state to state but had many features in common. In some states they forbade Negroes to own land; in many Negroes were forbidden to be on the streets at night; in most they were liable to be arrested if they left a job without permission of their employer—and their jail sentence would be to go back to work for him!

A representative of the Chamber of Commerce of New York, touring the South on a business survey, reported:

> These codes were simply the old black code of the state, with the word "slave" expunged and "Negro" substituted. The most odious features of slavery were preserved in them.

The writer also went on to say that he had been called upon, in the Deep South, by delegations of landowners who argued that the Emancipation Proclamation was illegal, and who hoped and expected that the Supreme Court would outlaw it and restore their slaves to them.

To Grant it began to seem as if the whole sacrifice of the war had been wasted. He recalled the words of his final salute to his troops: "By your patriotic devotion . . . you have maintained the supremacy of the Union and the Constitution, overthrown all armed opposition to the enforcement of the laws and of the proclamations forever abolishing slavery—the cause and pretext of the rebellion." He remembered well that these troops were one-fifth Negro at the war's end. In his sense of obligation to his former soldiers he was colorblind.

Worse than the reports of the Black Codes were the terrifying dispatches that came in through official Army channels. The picture they gave was one of persistent hostility and repeated widespread outbreaks of violence and cruelty to freedmen, particularly ex-soldiers. There were many instances of beatings and woundings, burnings and killings, and destruction of their pitifully small, recently acquired property, the fruit of their frugal earnings. Freedmen were not the sole victims. In many communities whites who had remained loyal to the Union suffered outrages. The state and local officials who had come into office as a result of Johnson's rapid, unconditional transfer of power to ex-Confederates refused to protect veterans or even United States Army personnel from insults and intermittent physical assaults. Grant joined with Secretary of War Stanton in protesting to the President, but the latter refused to interfere.

The people of the loyal states reacted strongly to the news of the atrocities in the South, the description of the Rebel-dominated state legislatures, and the repugnant features of the Black Codes. They feared that the sacrifices of the war were in vain and that its results would be undone. Many came to accept the views of the advanced thinkers, in and out of Congress, who were attacking Johnson and advocating national action to protect civil rights in all states.

To give the Southern Negro the right to vote and participate in government locally would not have been a popular measure in the spring of 1865. However, the developments in the South tended to make more and more people see the justice of the arguments of such men as Massachusetts Senator Charles Sumner and Pennsylvania Representative Thaddeus Stevens. These men had recognized, and brought a majority of people to see, that the Negro, once freed and allowed to fight to defend his freedom and his country, was entitled to have all the privileges of citizenship. This was practically what Grant had said to Eaton three years before.

When the new Congress met in December, 1865, it did so in a mood to act—the more so because during the war years the Presidency had, as inevitable during wartime, seized powers and taken steps without Congressional approval that would have been unthinkable in "normal" peacetime. Aside from the many unpleasant reports from the South, the fact that this was the first occasion on which

Congress, which had not met since March, could express its own ideas on the manner and conditions for restoring the defeated states, made it a crucial time for a new look at Andrew Johnson's program.

The Congress faced first the question of whether to seat the senators and representatives from the Johnson-reconstructed states. A resolution was adopted that exercised the constitutional right of Congress to pass on the qualifications of its own members by excluding the motley group of secessionists, ex-Confederate officers, and others until an investigation could be made of the true conditions under which the newcomers were elected. This was to turn out to be the first of the great congressional investigations which have since come to be so familiar.

Many witnesses were heard by the Joint Committee on Reconstruction, as Congress called this new group. The previous stories in the newspapers and in Army dispatches about force and violence that had been used against the poor freedmen were confirmed. Loyal white Southerners who had opposed secession were present and told how they were treated as outcasts, insulted, and threatened with floggings or lynchings. One United States District Judge had witnessed a Confederate army surgeon shoot and kill a man whose only offense was that he had voted for Lincoln in 1860. General George Custer, sent by Grant to Texas as the head of the garrison there, testified: "The people of the North have no conception of the murders that have been committed in Texas during and since the war. . . . It is of weekly, if not daily, occurrence that freedmen are murdered."

Early in 1866 a bill was passed to extend the life of the Freedmen's Bureau—the agency that Grant had warmly defended in his report to Johnson—and to enlarge its powers to secure equal rights and "exact and equal justice before the law." The bureau was the sole agency in existence that could enable an unprepared nation to discharge its obligations to guide and protect four million Americans in their transition from slavery to freedom. It was the central Government's first great experiment in administering a plan to aid the "general welfare." Its officials helped in the most important educational work among the former slaves; it aided them in the purchase or lease of lands; it protected them against oppressive labor contracts and biased state courts. It was the natural agency to be entrusted with the broad assignment of abolishing slavery not merely in word but in fact. One legislator who denounced the Black Codes against which the expanded Freedmen's Bureau Bill was directed summed it up: "It is idle to say that a man is free who cannot come and go at pleasure, who cannot buy and sell, who cannot enforce his rights."

The new bill passed by large majorities. When it came before President Johnson he denounced and vetoed it. This was the beginning of a breach between Congress and Johnson that was to grow wider. Johnson's veto was criticized by moderate and conservative newspapers as well as by those called "radical," that had consistently sponsored full emancipation. The Southern press, however, hailed Johnson's action triumphantly. "The old Tennessean has shown his blood," said one.

Shortly afterward, in a bitter tirade against freedom's spokesmen, at a public meeting, Johnson completed his rupture with Lincoln's Congress.

28

Replacing the Secretary of War

★★★★

PRESIDENT JOHNSON's break with Congress in February, 1866, touched off a great national debate that grew louder and more furious during the ensuing months and continued until the important midterm congressional elections of 1866. Grant's training and sense of discipline prevented him from taking sides openly in a purely political dispute. However, as General in Chief, he was more conscious than any other single American of the nature of developments in the former Rebel areas. Differing attitudes toward those events were at the heart of the Johnson-Congress conflict.

During the first difficult months of 1866 Grant hoped for a reconciliation of the differences between Johnson and the Congress. He could not help but be disturbed by information he received that indicated that the continuing stubborn combativeness of Johnson was arousing in the white South an appetite to regain its prewar domination over the country's affairs. Moreover, the President's opposition to the Freedmen's Bureau and Civil Rights Acts seemed to incite the worst elements of the former slaveholding areas. There was eliminated whatever slim hope existed that enlightened community leaders would begin the difficult task of readjusting race relations on the premise that the Negro was a human being. Racial prejudice and hostility was encouraged to re-emerge now that it seemed that a Johnson-led coalition would legitimitize the repression of the freedmen.

As the months passed, Grant became totally disillusioned with the President, and came to feel that his own chivalrous generosity to the white South and its leaders had been wasted. His heart hardened when he received dispatches such as the one about a soldier in uniform, a Negro sentry, who had been lynched by a mob in Knoxville, Tennessee, with no effort by local officials to interfere or to punish the guilty. He was disturbed and angry when he received a report of the formation of a new Virginia state militia, from which Negroes would be excluded, to be commanded by former Rebel officers. He became furious when Johnson forwarded to him a request for arms and equipment for this group, and he recommended to the Secretary of War that it be refused.

Johnson created a new problem for Grant, the Army, and the nation, by a decision in April, 1866, to declare the rebellion officially ended. The trouble with this was that conditions were still extremely unstable in the South, and veterans, Army personnel, and especially officials of the Freedmen's Bureau were constantly being harassed by local courts and public officials. The President's "peace" proclamations might terminate the Army's war powers, and raised doubt as to the legality of Grant's standing military orders that civil rights be protected by Federal courts or special courts set up by the bureau itself. This new crisis brought Congress to complete action on a proposed new amendment to the Constitution, that was to become the Fourteenth. The principal portion of the new amendment was to establish first-class citizenship for all Americans and to prohibit any state action that would deny the people equal protection of the laws. It was intended to destroy the legal foundations of racism in the United States.

The proposed amendment represented a sane and moderate solution to the two major problems of the postwar period: how to permit the former Confederate states to resume self-government and at the same time to keep the faith of the national Government with the men who fought to defend it on the promise that they were fighting for their own freedom as well. If Johnson's advisers had persuaded him to back the proposal, it might have helped repair the breach between Johnson and Congress and bring about the national unity essential to help solve the difficult and dangerous problems of Reconstruction. The way would have been opened for the Southern states to resume their place in the Union with dignity, while at the same time insuring Government protection of all citizens from the hostility and prejudice bequeathed by slavery.

Johnson refused to meet Congress halfway, opposed and even denounced the Fourteenth Amendment. It could not be expected that the white leaders of the South would accept the spirit or terms of the proposal if Lincoln's Vice-President did not. They, together with Johnson, looked forward to the 1866 elections as an opportunity to overthrow the existing majority in Congress.

During the 1866 campaign the President attempted to use Grant's popularity to help his faction. He asked the General to accompany him on his campaign tour. The scheme worked only to the extent of helping to draw crowds, who were hostile to Johnson but cheered Grant.

The people of Johnson's own home state demonstrated in a tragic way the effect of the President's incitation against the Civil Rights legislation and Constitutional amendment. In the late spring of 1866 there was a vicious and indiscriminate attack on the Negro population of Memphis. Forty-six men, women, and children were killed and more than eighty wounded. Only one white was injured.

This was followed by a massacre at New Orleans in the late summer of the same year. A mob began an attack on a convention of Negroes and whites, and then extended their attack on the Negro population of the city. Thirty-four Negroes were killed and more than two hundred were seriously injured; four white men lost their lives.

These incidents prompted Grant to take measures to protect against an attempt by Johnson to seize power and to establish a dictatorship. He notified General Sheridan, who was in command at New Orleans:

> I regret to say that since the unfortunate differences between the President and Congress, the former becomes more violent with the opposition he meets with, until now but few people who were loyal to the government during the rebellion seem to have any influence with him. I much fear that we are fast approaching the time that he will want to declare Congress itself unconstitutional and revolutionary. Commanders in the Southern states will have to take care and see if a crisis comes that no armed headway can be made against the Union.

The elections resulted in a decisive repudiation of Johnson and his program. The people's disapproval did not alter his course. He remained unwilling to attempt to work with Congress. He incited the Confederate-controlled state legislatures of the South to refuse to ratify the proposed Fourteenth Amendment. Grant at this point could not remain silent. He argued and pleaded with every Southerner who called on him at Washington, for the sake of the South and the sake of the country, to accept a peace based on racial justice. He believed, and told the Southerners, who were still grateful for his postwar compassion, that it was essential that they accept the Fourteenth Amendment, and that if they did so it would "much modify the demands that may be made if there is delay." His prophetic warning went unheeded.

Congress reconvened with the endorsement of the election returns and the stimulus of the rejection of the Fourteenth Amendment by the Johnson-created legislatures of the Confederate states. It resolved that it had to take matters into its own hands and start all over from the beginning in reconstructing the ex-Rebel areas. All of Johnson's actions in setting up the first crop of postwar governments were voided. New conventions in the states were to be held to insure the establishment of state constitutions and governments that would recognize civil and human rights. To make certain that they would do so, Congress imposed the condition that the right to vote for convention delegates should be extended to Negroes. No state would be readmitted until it had ratified the Fourteenth Amendment.

During the debate on the new Reconstruction laws, in response to a request from the Senate, Grant asked General O. O. Howard, the head of the Freedmen's Bureau, to collect authenticated case histories of lawlessness against Negroes and Federal officers in the South under the Johnson governments. The report submitted listed literally hundreds of acts of violence.

By the spring of 1867 Grant had come to agree with the Congress that the extension of the suffrage to the freedmen was the only means of securing and insuring the emancipation that had been won on the field of battle. He was in constant touch with congressional leaders now, and was consulted by them as they drew up the new laws. For his part, as he had stated in his report to Johnson, he would have preferred to keep the South under full military control until the victims of slavery were more fully prepared to use the ballot and the whites more thoroughly reconciled to the necessity of becoming partners in citizenship with those whom they had only recently ruled. Any hope of this type of transition had been destroyed by Johnson.

When Congress passed the new Reconstruction laws, they included one designed to protect Lincoln's appointees to Federal office, many of whom were being removed or threatened with removal by Johnson. The law was unusual, but so were the circumstances. With many officials under fire for merely executing the laws that Congress had passed over Johnson's veto, or being displaced by the new political machine that Johnson was trying to build, there was considerable justification for the extraordinary provision that Federal officials could not be removed by the President except with the consent of the Senate.

After the first session of the new Congress adjourned,

Johnson determined to suspend Secretary of War Stanton from office as a prelude to submitting the proposal to remove him to the next Senate. Stanton had been a brilliant lawyer who had joined Lincoln's Cabinet during the war, and by his dedication and energy helped to win the war. He had, as a member of the Cabinet, constantly warned Johnson against the course he had pursued. Now he was to be dropped. To make the removal more acceptable to the nation, Johnson decided to appoint Grant as acting Secretary of War. Grant protested, saying, "Removal of the Secretary of War cannot be effected against his will without the consent of the Senate. It was but a short time since the United States Senate was in session, and why not then have asked for his removal if it was then desired?"

Nevertheless, since Stanton's suspension while the Senate was in recess was legal, Grant agreed to accept the temporary appointment to avoid the imposition of a worse choice: possibly a civilian superior who might obstruct and sabotage enforcement of the Reconstruction laws.

29

From War Secretary to President

★★★★

EARLY IN 1867 United States Senator Benjamin Wade of Ohio started to look for a candidate for President to run on the Republican ticket in 1868. The Republicans were a very young party, and it was feared that they might still be in a minority, as they had been when they had elected Lincoln four years after their first national ticket was run. Wade and his fellow party leaders knew that Ulysses Grant was by far the most popular man in the country, but the soldier had kept his opinions so much to himself that they were not sure that he supported what were then the party's principles. How could they accept him as a candidate if they did not know what he stood for?

It occurred to Senator Wade that he might drop in to see Jesse Grant at Covington, Kentucky, across the river from his home state. Jesse's early antislavery views and letters to editors were still remembered, and Ben Wade hoped that Jesse would give him an idea as to where his son stood on the great issues of the day. Jesse and Hannah were out visiting when Wade arrived, but the Reverend M. J. Cramer, who was married to Ulysses' youngest sister, Mary, was there.

"Perhaps you can tell me what I want to know," said Wade, who had been recognized and received by Dr. Cramer. "I want to know what General Grant's sentiments are with regard to the Freedmen's Bureau, the Reconstruction Acts, and so on. We are thinking of nominating him for President and yet we do not know exactly where he stands on these questions."

"Well," replied the clergyman, "I know my brother-in-law's sentiments on all these great questions, but when he told me his opinions at a social gathering he exacted a promise that what he was saying would not go to the press. If you will keep it confidential, I will tell you what you want to know."

"Agreed," said the senator. His host then assured him that Grant supported the acts of Congress for the benefit of the freedmen, for the reconstruction of the Southern states, etc. When Cramer finished, the senator threw his great Western-style hat into the air—breaking one of the globes of the chandelier—and exclaimed, "That settles the matter; I am greatly relieved. He shall be our candidate, and with him we are sure to win."

Nevertheless there were many who did not understand General Grant's attitude during those months in the latter part of 1867 when he served as acting Secretary of War, and thereby seemed to be supporting Johnson's policies. A letter he had written protesting the suspension of Stanton had not been made public. The nation did not for a long time appreciate that he had kept the secretaryship from falling into the hands of one more subservient to Johnson. However, news of such conversations as that between Dr. Cramer and Senator Wade helped protect Grant's reputation during that difficult period. While Grant, despite Rawlins's and Julia's urging, was unwilling to consider himself, or be considered, as a Presidential candidate, he did not want his motives in acting as Secretary of War under Johnson to be misconstrued.

Grant carefully avoided participation in the purely political aspects of the Cabinet meetings that he was now required to attend. The routine duties of his new, additional position he performed conscientiously and with care. He kept the functions of his two positions distinct, and as Secretary of War would give orders to himself as General of the Army. He would visit both his old and his new office daily, and one of his aides remarked that at the War Office he was stiff and formal, as he thought a Cabinet member ought to be, while back at general headquarters he was a soldier at ease with his staff, intimate and unrestrained. As Secretary, he acted as he thought Secretary Stanton would act, and he turned down requests that Sam Grant, as Secretary in his own right, might have indulged.

Shortly after he became Acting Secretary of War, Grant came to the defense of General Sheridan when Johnson had determined to remove that gallant warrior from the command of the Louisiana-Texas military district. In Grant's opinion a firm hand like Sheridan's was badly needed in New Orleans, where the local officials had connived in the August massacre. Johnson insisted on ousting the popular general. Grant responded in a letter requesting that Sheridan be allowed to continue in his post: "It is the will of the country that General Sheridan should not be removed from his present command." By this he meant, of course, that a majority of the people had approved at the polls the policies that Sheridan was being punished for enforcing. Johnson replied with sarcasm and technical correctness, "I am not aware that the question of retaining General Sheridan in command of the Fifth Military District has ever been submitted to the people themselves for determination."

In his discomfiture at this exchange Grant could have learned that he was not as fit for controversy as for command. His old friend Sherman had come East on a trip only a short time before and urged him to stay out of politics. One of his own staff (history, with a strange sense of fatal irony records that it was Colonel Babcock, who was later to help put Grant's Administration under a cloud) wrote to Grant's early patron, Congressman Elihu Washburne: "I am one of those who hope that General Grant will not be President. I look upon it as a great misfortune to him."

The politicians thought otherwise, and the popular sentiment that began to show itself did not have to be artificially stimulated. "Grant for President" clubs began to be formed in many Northern cities. Businessmen, anxious for a restoration of harmony between the sections of the country, backed the drive, tired and disgusted by the bickering and bitterness that were the result of Andrew Johnson's Administration. Johnson's term of office almost ended a year sooner than scheduled. The idea of "impeaching"—the Constitutional method of removing—the President had been considered shortly after the violent breach between Johnson and Lincoln's last Congress. The talk of removing President Johnson became more active after the new Congress elected in 1866 had met, especially when it was feared that he was sabotaging proper administration of the Reconstruction laws. The issue came to a head when, after the new session of Congress convened at the end of 1867, the Senate disapproved Johnson's removal of Stanton and ordered him reinstated under the Tenure of Office Act. This law had been passed to protect from Johnson's wrath officials who administered the laws that Congress passed over his veto.

Ulysses Grant was directly involved in the events leading up to the impeachment charges. When he learned that the Senate had rejected removal of Stanton, he quietly turned the keys of the Secretary's office over to the man he had been temporarily replacing. Johnson had requested that Grant stay on as Acting Secretary until the courts passed on the legality of the Senate's action. He declared that Grant promised that he would. Grant's denial resulted in a bitter dispute between General and President. Johnson's repeated statements involved the good faith of Grant and his honor. Grant bitterly broke off all personal relations with the President, writing him:

> . . . you must have known that my greatest objection to Mr. Stanton's removal or suspension was the fear that some one would be appointed in his stead, who would, by opposition to the laws relating to the restoration of the Southern states to their proper relations to the Government, embarrass the Army in the performance of duties especially imposed upon it by these laws; and it was to prevent such an appointment that I accepted the office of Secretary of War *ad interim,* and not for the purpose of enabling you to get rid of Mr. Stanton by my withholding it from him in opposition to law. . . .
>
> And now Mr. President, when my honor as a soldier and integrity as a man have been so violently assailed, pardon me for saying that I can but regard this whole matter from the beginning to the end, as an attempt to involve me in the resistance of law . . . and thus to destroy my character before the country.

Very shortly afterwards the House of Representatives impeached—that is, accused—Johnson of offenses requiring his removal from office. Never before (or since) had a President of the United States stood so accused. Grant had been averse to the idea of impeaching Johnson when the subject was first brought up in Grant's presence in 1866. However, when the crisis finally arrived, he heartily approved the action. The controversy with Johnson, more than any other single factor, resulted in his yielding to the temptation of running for the Presidency.

The United States Senate acts as a court to determine if an official should be removed after he has been impeached. The impeachment trial was probably the most dramatic episode in its history. Removal—that is, a finding of guilt—requires a two-thirds majority and Johnson escaped by a margin of one vote. Historians have often doubted whether political disagreement, no matter how bitter and protracted, was ever intended to justify removal of a President. Whether or not they are correct in belittling the actual charges that were leveled against Johnson, the charge for which he must answer to history remains: that through his stubbornness and incompetence as a national leader Andrew Johnson destroyed an opportunity to remove the stain of three centuries of slavery, and lost the chance to create national unity for the postwar years based on justice, human rights, and racial readjustment. No law passed over his veto, no matter how well enforced, could remedy the damage he did to Southern Americans by making them believe and hope that white supremacy could be preserved, and inciting them to fight, illegally, to preserve it.

Toward the end of the impeachment trial, during a recess, the national Republican nominating convention was held in Cincinnati. There Ulysses S. Grant was named unanimously as candidate for President. He received the first news of the nomination from former Secretary Stanton. He took it in the same way that he had received every important announcement of his life—with that calm self-restraint that made it possible for him to keep his mind on the problem at hand during the heat of every battle. "There was no shade of exultation or agitation on his face, not a flush on his cheek, nor a flash in his eye," wrote Colonel Badeau, an old friend who had acted as his military secretary. Those around him doubted that he felt elated, and there was little reason indeed for anyone to be overjoyed. Certainly the task that he would face if elected was more difficult than any President had faced in his century. To win a peace is more difficult than to win a war. To restore a country torn by civil war, changed in character by the tremendous power of emerging industrialism, swamped by a torrent of greed and speculation, and to undo the harm that Johnson had done—all this would have been an enormously difficult task for a seasoned and capable politician and statesman.

For this essentially quiet and self-contained man who knew how to command but not how to persuade, it was too much. He had been told so often that he was indispensable

BETTMANN ARCHIVE

General Grant and his family leave Galena, Illinois for Washington on November 7, 1868, after his election as President.

to the country that one might expect him by now to believe it. He voiced the sentiment in the heart of every American in his formal acceptance statement in four words that seized the country's imagination and became his campaign slogan: "Let us have peace."

He refused from the very first to take any active part in the campaign. He had some idea of the problems he faced and thought that only if he was chosen for office by demand of the people, without promise or commitment by himself, could he succeed. The party managers were annoyed by this approach. His friends thought it unwise, but he could not be persuaded to change. He went off to Galena to "sit it out." Rawlins remained in the East, in touch with the party managers, but this did not soothe their feelings, and as it was to turn out, the Grant Administration started with an additional unnecessary handicap in the hostility of many of his own party.

On the evening of election day, November, 1868, he went to Congressman Washburne's house, where a direct connection with the telegraph had been hooked up so that he could follow the returns. Every man present seemed more excited than the candidate. When the news of his election seemed definite, he walked up the Galena hill and kissed Julia, who had waited up.

"I'm afraid I am elected," he said a bit sadly.

30

No Chance for Victory

★★★★

"A MESSAGE from the President of the United States," announced the clerk of the Senate. The senators, as usual, began to yawn, to read newspapers, to drift out of the chamber in groups of two and three so that they could talk business or politics in the anterooms.

It was eight years after Ulysses had walked up the hill at Galena to give the news of his election to Julia and the children. As the afternoon began on this December 5, 1876, the clerk began to read aloud the President's last annual message to the Congress.

"It was my fortune, or misfortune, to be called to the office of Chief Executive without any previous political training. From the age of seventeen I had never even witnessed the excitement attending a Presidential campaign but twice antecedent to my own candidacy, and at but one of them was I eligible as a voter."

By this time the chamber was more than three-quarters empty. For the most part no disrespect was intended. The senators could read it later, and they did not care for the clerk's monotonous delivery.

"Under such circumstances it is but reasonable to suppose that errors of judgment must have occurred. . . . Mistakes have been made, as all can see and I admit, but it seems to me oftener in the selections made of the assistants appointed to aid in carrying out the various duties of administering the Government. . . . It is impossible, where so many trusts are to be alloted, that the right parties should be chosen in every instance. History shows that no Administration from the time of Washington to the present has been free from these mistakes. But I leave comparisons to history, claiming only that I have acted in every instance from a conscientious desire to do what was right, constitutional, within the law, and for the very best interests of the whole people. Failures have been errors of judgment, not of intent."

Those frank and self-critical words were Grant's own. Unlike Andrew Johnson, and some later Presidents, Grant insisted on writing his own speeches and messages. No one, in any case, except the President himself would close his Administration with such a straightforward confession of "errors" and "mistakes."

He had learned much since that Inauguration Day in March, 1869, that had dawned so cold and rainy. Washington seemed full of Dents and Grants—except for his mother who was too shy to come. The sun had broken through the clouds as Grant and Rawlins had joined the parade to the Capitol, and that seemed a good omen. The new President felt stiff and uncomfortable in the black dress suit that he had bought to replace the uniform taken off only the day before. He had not wanted to resign as commanding general until Inauguration Day: he knew it was important for the things he believed in that Johnson should not be allowed to appoint a new commander.

He had worked hard and prepared carefully for that first Inauguration in 1869, and the speech had seemed to go well. "The responsibilities of the position I feel, but accept them without fear." Some had thought those words too immodest; those who knew Grant well felt their sincerity. "The office has come to me unsought; I commence its duties untrammeled." This was so true that the politicians winced as he said it. He had not campaigned; he had not asked their advice before or on election day; as Inauguration Day drew near, he had not even consulted, as far as any of them knew, on the all-important question of who should make up his Cabinet.

As he looked out upon the sea of faces in the crowd that was massed on that cold but now sunny day, he could see that more than half of them were Negroes—citizens by reason of the adoption of the Fourteenth Amendment, but still without any protection of the right to vote. He placed great emphasis on the last recommendation at the end of his short inaugural address:

"The question of suffrage is one which is likely to agitate the public so long as a portion of the citizens of the nation are excluded from its privileges in any state. It seems to me very desirable that this question should be settled now, and I entertain the hope and express the desire that it may be by ratification of the fifteenth article of amendment to the Constitution."

Four score and thirteen years had passed since the nation had been founded; it was his privilege and opportunity to be the President who was urging the people to make a reality, in their Constitution, of the words of their Declaration of Independence . . . all men created equal; government by the consent of the governed.

As he finished the speech he walked over to Julia and took her hand. "And now, my dear, I hope you're satisfied." This he said with a twinkle in his eye, because more than once during the anxious weeks before Inauguration Day she had urged him to consult Roscoe Conkling, the silver-tongued senator from New York, or one of the party's other great orators, for advice on how to write and deliver a speech. He had refused this, as he had rejected a speech by A. R. Corbin, his sister's fiancé. Corbin, a minor Wall Street figure, had presented one day a complete draft of an inaugural address, only to hear Grant sternly order that it be put out of sight.

He had kept his own counsel on the selection of his Cabinet. Once he said in jest that he got up several times a night to make sure that Julia had not peeked in his vest pocket to see what his selections were. Great interest and curiosity were aroused when, unlike every President before and since, he had declined to confer with anyone, even the men he had in mind for the posts, before making his Cabinet selections.

This, however, turned out badly. Several of his choices were not interested in the appointment and had to be pressed to accept it; one proved to be ineligible by law. The differences between the job of President of the United States and General of the Army were beginning to be more clear. A general keeps his own counsel and makes his important decisions on the spur of the moment. He selects his staff from among men whom he has the right to command. He need not worry whether they will accept the job or be approved by someone else when they are selected. He need not be concerned when he chooses a course of action about persuading a body of men that his decisions are the correct ones. No art of conciliation is needed: he is to produce results, or he will be replaced.

But the trouble was not merely that Ulysses Grant had been trained to think and act as a soldier. In the whole history of the United States there was only one other President who came to office with as little experience or familiarity with law or politics or the nature of constitutional government in a democracy. This was not necessarily fatal to the hopes of the country for a successful administration. No man is really qualified to be President of the United States before he becomes one; Grant had the will to learn the requirements of his job; he certainly entered office with the good wishes and approval of most of the people. His success in bringing the heartbreaking Civil War to an end and his willingness to treat the defeated with a spirit of forgiveness and understanding had made him by far the most popular man in the country, and perhaps the most popular that had ever entered the White House except for George Washington himself.

The obstacles were too great. No man could have been a wholly successful President of the United States in 1869.

It was not just the political mess that had been left by the Johnson Administration—although that had a great deal to do with it. Four years of wartime assumption of power by Lincoln, followed by four years of combat between Congress and the President during Johnson's term, had left the Congress, particularly the United States Senate, in a state of jealous watchfulness, and even the start of an administration of a President sympathetic to the majority of the senators could not change the habits of thought and attitudes of most of them.

Nor was the trouble primarily the unsettled condition of the ex-Rebel states that were gradually being readmitted to the Union under the congressional plan of Reconstruction that had been passed over Johnson's repeated stubborn vetoes. That trouble alone would have been enough to occupy the full time and attention of the greatest and wisest of statesmen; and yet even a man with Lincoln's great genius and human understanding would hardly have been able to repair the damage done during Johnson's Administration. Before Lincoln died, when the war had just been won and prewar Southern leaders were in a submissive mood, they might have been gently but firmly led to understand that the price of peace was a readjustment of race relationships based on recognition of full human rights for all. A united nation could have properly and fairly pointed out that 200,000 Negro soldiers who had made the difference between defeat and victory in the war for survival of the nation—and who had proved their manhood by their performance—could not be let down, and the white South might have listened and learned.

However, when Johnson and most of his Cabinet parted company with the Congress on the Freedmen's Bureau and Civil Rights bills, the white South was needlessly encouraged to believe that by continuing its stubborn resistance to racial justice there could be preserved a way of life that made it possible for one part of the population to benefit from a status "superior" to that of another part of the population. Before the war they called it slavery; now they called it "keeping the Negro in his place," and later they were to call it segregation. With the North war-weary and about to re-charge racial prejudice, the opportunity thrown away during Johnson's time could not easily be re-created.

The political problems and the turmoil in the South that Andrew Johnson had left were not the worst. More serious and more devastating in their effects on Grant's Presidency were two forces that had appeared during the sixties and now dominated. The one was big business and the other corruption, and they were linked by a third force, a mania for speculation and getting rich quick. The harmful effects of the stunning growth of big business were to be first felt in an adverse way during Grant's Administration, but that growth did not start then: it started almost simultaneously with the war, or slightly before. Unleashed on a huge scale by the necessities of the war, rapid business expansion continued afterwards throughout Johnson's term of office.

The nation borrowed three billions of dollars—an immense sum then—to finance the war, and had to pay heavy interest on the loan. The money borrowed was spent quickly. Contractors and brokers, who furnished the goods that the nation needed, were able to make fortunes, many of them honestly and many not. There was plenty of money for investment and more for speculation—gambling in the prices of stocks, of gold, of commodities. The character of the moral fabric of the country changed tremendously, not only because of the blood and hate and cruelty that comes with war, but because of the prospects of a golden and easy future to be gotten, not as the pioneers did—by crossing into the wilderness, by sacrifice and hard work—but by quick thinking and shrewd manipulation.

This was the national moral climate when Grant became President. He did not bring it with him or produce it; it was there, ready made, and a difficult condition to cope with. In addition there were regional tendencies that had developed unchecked and without much opposition. In Northern cities there appeared a new breed of corrupt and wicked politicians who based their power on a distortion of democracy: the manipulation of the votes of unfortunate, uneducated immigrants. Most notorious was "Boss" Tweed of the New York Democrats.

The South had been plagued before the war with intermittent misappropriation of public funds. In Mississippi, for example, in 1839 less than one-tenth of the money collected by local sheriffs and court clerks in fines and forfeitures ever reached the treasury of the state. In 1840 there were twenty-six county tax collectors who were listed as having misappropriated at least $1,000 each. In 1858 the State auditor himself made off with $54,000. Jefferson College had an endowment fund of almost a quarter of a million dollars which literally disappeared. Altogether, in the years before the Civil War, there were misappropriations by state officials in Tennessee, Georgia, Louisiana, Texas, Alabama, and Arkansas, as well as Mississippi, that ran into large sums.

These were some of the domestic conditions that Grant faced when he became President of the United States.

31

The Great Gold Conspiracy

★★★★

THE GAMBLING FEVER that had caused so much stock and commodity speculation had continued after the end of the war. There was this difference: in wartime the rise and fall of prices sometimes depended on news of the loss or gain of a battle, or the capture of a city, or the crossing of a river. In cases where the outcome depended on the fortunes of war, the professional of Wall Street and the amateur investors were on roughly equal terms. Neither was qualified to forecast these events or to influence their outcome.

When the war ended and Andrew Johnson became President, the advantage went to the men, mostly in the great brokerage houses, who were experienced in the tricks that sometimes made it possible to influence the rise or fall of stock prices. The growth of larger and larger corporations, and the issuance of their shares to raise capital, resulted in a far greater volume of trading and speculating than had ever been seen in this country. The very largest corporations in those days were the railroads, which were growing at an almost unbelievable rate of speed. The greatest of these, and therefore most tempting to the machinations of crafty speculators, was the Erie Railroad, which, after almost being wrecked in a fight for control between Cornelius Vanderbilt and Daniel Drew, fell into the hands of Jay Gould and James Fisk.

Gould was a stockbroker and a gambler with no ethics and yet was, according to the historian of those times, Henry Adams, "as honest as the mass of his fellows" on Wall Street. His colleague Fisk, a flamboyant, reckless fellow, had started life as a peddler and ended up as a successful and equally unethical speculator. Gould and Fisk took over the Erie while Johnson was still President, and although they did not own all or even most of the stock, they were able to control its affairs. It was run as a private empire, its money used to buy a New York opera house for a plush headquarters and its influence used to increase the prestige of the men who had secured control. Late in 1868 Gould and Fisk added to the Erie's board of directors "Boss" Tweed and Peter B. Sweeney, leaders of Tammany Hall, the New York City Democratic organization.

Not content with their local power, and greedy for greater wealth, Gould and Fisk began to dream of a scheme of "cornering" the gold market in New York. Gold was dealt in openly and legally as both a commodity and a currency at that time, its price fluctuating because there were still in circulation millions of dollars of "greenbacks" (money not redeemable in gold) that had been issued to help pay the staggering costs of the Civil War. There was always a legitimate need for gold, for payment of customs duties and foreign payments, and this market created an opportunity for speculation. However, apart from the national Government's hoard of the precious metal, there was never more than a limited supply at hand, which in those days could not be quickly affected by shipments from Europe or Africa. If control over the limited New York supply could be secured, the price could be forced up and up and a tremendous fortune, a "killing," could be made at the expense of those who might have speculatively contracted to sell gold that they did not yet own. The success or failure of such a grandiose scheme depended on either control or prediction of the actions of the national Government, which might at any moment affect the market by buying or selling gold. Gould and Fisk set about to attempt to influence what the Government might do. Fortunately for their purposes, they had access to Abel Rathbone Corbin, a semi-retired speculator now on the fringe of Wall Street, who had married Ulysses Grant's sister "Jennie"—Virginia.

In June of 1869, three months after he had become President, Grant dropped in to see Jennie and Corbin in New York on his way to attend a Peace Jubilee in Boston. Gould persuaded Corbin to invite him to his house to meet the President; while there he was able to prevail upon Ulysses and Julia to be guests of the Erie on one of the fine new steamboats that were used by the company between New York and Boston. There was nothing unusual, discreditable, or irregular in this, for Gould and Fisk were considered respectable capitalists who enjoyed the privilege of extending hospitality to a President without any adverse comment. (For the occasion, Fisk wore, with the utmost seriousness, a blue uniform, a broad gilt capband, and three silver stars on his coatsleeves. It was the privilege of a civilian official of a corporation that owned a civilian ship to appoint himself commodore aboard her.)

In preparing for their attempt at a coup on the gold market, Gould and Fisk had worked up a theory about the relation of the price of gold to the movement of crops from West to East on the Erie Railroad. Perhaps they even had come to believe it themselves. In any case, it did more than give them an excuse to use the Erie's assets for their shenanigans. It sounded patriotic. They tested their theory on the President during dinner on their steamboat, as the ship sliced through the choppy waters of Long Island Sound. Corbin sat listening with great interest and attention, while Julia remained preoccupied with her dinner and the beautiful view of the Connecticut shore.

"London is still the center of the world's wheat market," said Gould, "and the price there controls the New York price. If gold prices go up, the dollar is cheaper in London and wheat prices higher in Chicago. Our surplus wheat will then be able to compete with European wheat in the London market." The President frowned. He was not sure that he understood what they were trying to say, and Corbin, sensing this, and not wanting Grant to suspect that he was being used, changed the subject.

Later in the summer Corbin met with Gould and Fisk, who had enlisted his continued interest by buying gold in his name so that he would benefit from a rise in price. They tried this with General Horace Porter, too, a secretary to the President, but he angrily refused to accept it. Unfortunately he did not tell the President of the attempt.

"Don't give up because he sounded discouraging on the boat," said the brother-in-law to the speculators. "It's his way when he's not sure. When he realizes that it's for the advantage of the farmers and the country, he'll tell Secretary of the Treasury Boutwell to hold on to the Government gold while you bid the price up."

Gould and Fisk had already started to make purchases through secret agents, and their ambition would not have let them stop, in any case. They went on with their plans and late in August formed a "pool" or group of speculators, who started to buy gold steadily during the last days of August. The group managed, somehow, to have an editorial "planted" in *The New York Times*, stating that the Government would not interfere in the gold market.

Much of that first summer of his Presidency, Ulysses and Julia spent in travel. Not only did they go on the trip to Boston, but later to West Point, where their son Fred was a cadet, and still later to the then highly fashionable New York resort at Saratoga Springs. As the city of Washington grew larger, it became a less and less comfortable place to stay during the summer; moreover, the President really was, after all, the boy grown up who always had taken the greatest pleasure in traveling great distances over the countryside.

There was nothing remarkable about his summer relaxation or travels, especially as the development of the telegraph had made it possible for him to keep in constant touch with Washington. However, the growing group that was looking for aspects of Grant's Administration to criticize was to seize upon his absences.

During that summer Abel Corbin had used every chance he could to impress Gould's crop theories upon the President. In early September, moved by the sincere belief that the economy of the nation would benefit, Grant, during a visit to the Corbins' on his way to Saratoga, allowed himself to be convinced. "It is my opinion," he wrote the Secretary of the Treasury, "that it is undesirable to force down the price of gold. It is important to the West that they should be able to move their crops at this time of the year."

The price of gold began to climb in the early days of September. The scheme to "corner" the market and make a killing had not come off yet, however, due to a successful counteroffensive by the "bears" of Wall Street—speculating groups interested in forcing prices back down. Gould, who had carried the gamble almost alone until then, called on Fisk for help, and the latter made heavy purchases through his own brokerage house. Then, on September 12, the President passed through New York again and this time, while he was at Corbin's house, told his brother-in-law, after a visit by Gould, "This is the last time I want you to let in Gould while I'm here."

The President went off to a quiet little mountain retreat in western Pennsylvania for a few days of peace and fresh air. Meanwhile in New York Gould, worried about his cool reception by Grant at Corbin's, and nervous about the tremendous size of his commitments, went too far. He induced Corbin, over whom he had a hold as a result of the investment he had made for him, to write an urgent letter to his brother-in-law, pleading with him to keep the Government's gold policy unchanged. Fisk took the letter and gave it to a special messenger employed by the Erie, who traveled many hours by rail and carriage until he arrived, dust-covered and weary, at the mountain resort. There he saw Grant and General Porter relaxing at a game of croquet on the lawn. The messenger dared not interrupt. At last, when the game was over and the men walked toward the house, he handed the envelope to Porter.

When the President and Porter came out of the house, the messenger tipped his hat. "Is it all right?" he asked. "All right," answered the President absently, meaning that he had been given the letter by Porter and read it. The messenger hastened to the nearest telegraph station and wired Fisk: "Delivered. All right." Naturally Fisk took this to mean that their plot would go on without interference by the Treasury Department, and the plungers went on to increase their commitments.

Not only was the messenger mistaken, but he had given away the plot! The President had at first supposed that he was a postman and the letter an ordinary piece of mail. When he realized from the man's waiting around that he was a special messenger, who had carried Corbin's message all the way from New York, his suspicions were aroused. Why should Corbin go to the trouble of hiring a special messenger to carry a letter from New York City?

When he realized that something was wrong, he did not see the full picture at first. But he could guess that Corbin had been speculating on the market: why else go to such trouble? He went in to Julia and said sternly, "I want you to write a letter to Jennie."

"Yes, dear, what about?"

"You must tell her to make her fool husband get out of the stock market. He's got no right to mix into things like that now."

On the morning of Wednesday, September 22, Jennie showed the letter to Abel. It was a bitter blow to him. "My husband," Julia had written to Jennie, "is annoyed by your husband's speculations." He could not understand it, when only a few days before there had been the wire that everything was "all right."

He went to Gould and asked that his share be sold out and that he be given his profit. "I've got to tell Grant I'm out of the market," he said, "and if you know him, then you know that when I do, it had better be the truth." Gould looked at him with the contemptuous look that men such as he reserve for weaker men whom they use for their own advantage. He wrote out a check and rushed down to the market.

Gould knew that by the time the President returned to Washington and heard how things were going on the Street that week, the game would be up. He decided that it was more important that he get out quietly, and with a whole skin, than that he let Fisk know of the disaster that impended!

Meanwhile Fisk was appearing daily in the section of the Stock Exchange called the Gold Room. He was buying wildly, roaring out his orders. Up and up went the price, which had been 130 when the plot started. It passed 160, the highest it had been since the last bad day of the war, and climbed to 162. Importers and others who had legitimate need of gold crowded in, frantic to buy. The rumor got around that Fisk had boasted he would have it up to 200 that Friday, September 23. The streets outside were filled with excited people, the small speculators as well as the morbidly curious. The telegraph offices could not keep up with the messages containing orders to buy or sell or requesting information; the whole nation, for the first time in its history, practically stopped to watch what the outcome would be.

Then the bubble burst. No one ever knew whether it was because of the telegram from Washington saying that the Treasury was putting gold on the market, or whether it was because news of Gould's sales began to get around. The hollow structure of speculation collapsed like a house of cards. In fifteen minutes the price was down to 132 and Black Friday had earned its name. Brokers failed, their firms and names were swept away. Speculators who had had unbelievable profits a few minutes before faced fantastic losses, which were paid off, in some cases, with suicide. The economy of the nation was shaken, but its momentum was strong enough to save it from tumbling then. Fisk, like a cat that always lands on its feet, survived, and no doubt calculating that he would have done the same in Gould's place, forgave and rejoined him.

There was little public outcry. It was to be another sixty years before abuses piled up sufficiently to bring about Federal regulation of the securities markets to attempt to prevent such episodes. Congress investigated Black Friday and how it came about, and President Grant was fully exonerated. But it was the first of a number of instances where he had misjudged men in political life. The General's gift of knowing a good soldier to entrust with a job did not seem to extend to civilian administration.

32

Santo Domingo Fiasco

★★★★

FROM THE DAYS when the thirteen original colonies united to become a nation, until the beginning of the Grant Administration in 1869, the most outstanding principle of our country's foreign policy had been expansion: the acquisition and absorption of neighboring territory. When the westward movement ceased at the shores of the Pacific before the Civil War, the eyes of the expansionists turned both north and south.

A move of importance in the direction of the north was taken during Johnson's Administration when Seward, Lincoln's Secretary of State, who had been held over by the new President, acquired Alaska from the Russian Czar. The public laughed and the newspapers fumed about the purchase of $7,000,000 worth of icebergs and Eskimos. Much of the opposition came from the papers who favored Johnson. It was the President's greatest enemy, Thaddeus Stevens, leader of the House of Representatives, who helped put through the bill to raise the money to pay for Alaska.

Ulysses Grant's boyhood near the frontier strongly influenced his attitude toward national expansion by means of territorial acquisition. He had seen the country grow northward and westward, and in the Mexican War he was an unwilling part of an aggressive seizure of territory to the southwest. When he became President, the expansionists were no longer the would-be settlers. Instead it was the traders and investors who looked to new territory. Their eyes were turned southeast, across the Gulf of Mexico. For one thing, there was a Cuban revolution against Spanish domination which stirred the idealism of some and the greed of others. There was also, between the Spanish island possessions of Cuba and Puerto Rico, the semitropical isle of Hispaniola. The island was divided into the Republic of Haiti, formerly held by the French, and the Dominican Republic, the former Spanish area of Santo Domingo. Both of these little nations had gained their independence before Grant became President.

The Dominican Republic was in a state of almost chronic civil war. Control of the country swung back and forth between two rival leaders, Baez and Cabral, neither of whom could remain in power long. Baez regained control in 1868 and was persuaded by some American traders and settlers that the way to solve both his political and his financial problems was by annexation to the United States. He sent an emissary to Washington, who managed to gain admission to the White House to present his offer to sell his own country.

President Grant, in office only a short time, listened with interest to the proposal. The picture of the fertility and the resources of the island was impressive and he was assured and believed that the people would like nothing better than to become a part of the United States. Grant knew the growing importance of sea power on the world stage, and had been troubled by the fact that every country in Europe had a naval base in the West Indies and that the United States, whose security most depended on it, did not. He was tempted, too, by the ambition of having his Administration marked by an important territorial acquisition—especially since the limits of continental expansion had been reached.

Ulysses Grant, experienced soldier, had not been a success in commercial enterprise during his Hardscrabble years and had no experience at all as a politician. He was not accustomed to expect chicanery and selfish trickery in others, and did not suspect or stop to inquire what might be wrong with the motives of a man like Baez, or of those who had persuaded him to peddle his country. Grant, moreover, was accustomed to devising his own strategy (very often on intuition and impulse) and he approached the Santo Domingo question as if it were a military problem which required for solution only his decision as to what the right course must be. What he did not see was that it was a political problem involving the study of all arguments and points of view, the art of persuasion, and compromise and adjustment.

After his own quick and favorable initial reaction to Baez's proposition, Grant did not consult his Cabinet or congressional leaders, but promptly sent one of his private secretaries (who had been a member of his military staff) to investigate conditions on the island. It was hardly four months after Grant had become President that General Orville Babcock, who had been a first-rate military engineer, but who was to be an embarrassing White House aide, set sail for Santo Domingo. Six weeks later he signed a draft of a treaty with the Dominican authorities, which provided for United States annexation of the island, something which he had not been given authority to do.

Babcock returned from the island full of enthusiasm, with traveling bags full of samples of its products. At the first Cabinet meeting after his return he was present, together with a display of the many specimens of ore and fruit from the island, and talked to whoever would listen about the virtues of annexation. The President was overjoyed and thought that he had accomplished the first great stroke of his Administration. He opened the meeting of the Cabinet with a smile.

"Babcock has returned, as you see," he said, "and has brought a treaty of annexation. I suppose it is not formal, as he had no diplomatic powers; but we can easily cure that. We can send back the treaty and have an officer of the State Department sign it, and that would make it all right."

There followed an embarrassing silence that was broken by Secretary of the Interior Cox, who asked, "But, Mr. President, has it been settled, then, that we want to annex Santo Domingo?"

The Secretary of State, Hamilton Fish, was silent and kept his eyes down. He had never liked the scheme and had not been in on it. There was no further response from anyone, and the silence became painful for Grant, who was not used to that sort of withholding of approval. He changed the subject.

Grant was surprised and angry. It was not the first time that he had learned as President that a decision would not be accepted merely because he had made it. As a general he might listen for hours to his staff, but when the time for talk was over, and the general gave a command, everybody moved and did his part in carrying it out. It was difficult to get used to the new state of things. Grant was sure that he was right, and he could not understand why others would disagree with his decision. As the days and weeks passed, the question of annexation of the island became a preoccupation with him.

He did not present it further at Cabinet meetings. He sent Babcock back with formal authority to enter into a treaty. Of course such a treaty had to be ratified by the United States Senate to become effective, and the battle over ratification led to a tragic split among the President's followers that was to mar and make even more difficult the rest of his Administration.

When Grant was elected President, the outstanding member of the United States Senate was Charles Sumner of Massachusetts. No mere politician, but a statesman in the old-fashioned sense of the word and a scholar and a humanitarian, Sumner had been the chief congressional spokesman for the slave before emancipation and for the freedman afterwards. He was widely known and respected as one who was inflexible in support of the moral principles in which he believed, and his personal and official integrity were above all question. Before the war, when he was the leading spokesman of the antislavery minority in Congress, Sumner was the victim of a cowardly physical assault on the United States Senate floor by a cane-wielding congressman from a slave state. The Massachusetts senator returned to the Congress, after having been long disabled, to become a pillar of Lincoln's Administration and chairman of the Senate Foreign Relations Committee, its most important group.

Ulysses Grant and Charles Sumner had similar aspirations and ideals, but they were quite unlike each other as human beings. They had only one resemblance: each possessed a stubborn determination to do what he thought was right, and distrusted and disliked those who might disagree with him. Sumner, as a scholar and student of world history had a tendency to distrust Grant, feeling that merely to have been a soldier was no qualification at all to lead a civilian democratic government. In this he may have been quite right, but his feelings were accented by a certain sense of disappointment that he had not himself been chosen to lead the country. Grant, on the other hand, had come to admire Sumner as a great idealist leader—and then to distrust and fear him slightly, as is the tendency of a man of action in the presence of a man of books and oratorical achievement.

During the last two years of Johnson's Administration, Grant and Sumner had been allies in the effort to rebuild the nation on the basis of equal rights and equal treatment for all citizens. Grant's point of view was that of the soldier who had seen the services of Negro troops and Southern white loyalists in helping to save the country and win the war; Sumner's was that of the humanist, the man who recognized, long before most of his fellow countrymen, that all men are brothers and that any disadvantage imposed upon a man's rights or opportunities by reason of the color of his skin was immoral and sinful. They were both members of the same party, and their unity and teamwork would have been valuable to the future of America. Unfortunately Grant and Sumner never got along well personally, and had started to drift apart at the very beginning of Grant's Administration because of Sumner's insistence on continuing laws passed by Congress to curb Johnson.

Shortly before Christmas of 1869 General Babcock returned from his second trip to Santo Domingo with a formal treaty of annexation. To become effective the treaty had to be ratified by the United States Senate. Since Senator Sumner was not only the outstanding figure in the Senate, but chairman of the Foreign Relations Committee that would consider the matter and make its recommendations, his attitude was sure to be a key factor.

Swallowing his pride—as he later said, for the only time in his life—because of his keen desire to accomplish this peaceful annexation of new territory, the President left the White House one day and strolled over to Sumner's apartment.

Sumner received the President with great courtesy and over a cup of tea they began to talk. Grant came right to the point and asked Sumner's help.

"I haven't seen the treaty yet," parried the Senator.

"I'll send it over tomorrow," promised Grant, and he went on to extol the virtues of his plan.

Sumner and Grant differed violently later about the last part of their talk. It has never been established whether Sumner promised to support the treaty, as Grant claimed, or merely that he would "consider" it. He did become the leader of the opposition, after having given full consideration to the President's arguments. He was, like many others, skeptical of the circumstances in which the treaty was negotiated; he suspected the motives of the Americans who had advised Dominican President Baez; he did not like the idea of the destruction of the independence of a little republic in which Negroes were a large part of the population. To

Grant it did not seem that way at all; and one of the great early leaders of the Negro people, Frederick Douglass, who respected and loved Sumner as "the most clearsighted, brave, and uncompromising friend" of his race, believed that Grant's move would benefit both the people of the United States and of Santo Domingo.

As Grant learned of the growth of the opposition to ratification of the Santo Domingo treaty in the Senate, he became more and more determined to try to push it through. He used his personal influence on the issue to an extent greater than any President ever had before on any measure. He was not accustomed to accept the idea of defeat or retreat. The less idealistic and more selfish politicians in his own party were the most loyal to him, and they advised him to use his power of appointment to Federal office as a method of influencing the doubtful senators to vote favorably. Even less in keeping with his own sense of integrity and honor was his reluctant request of the resignation of his Attorney General to win the votes of senators who had been offended by the Attorney General's policies.

All failed. The treaty was defeated. The damage to the President's prestige was greater than it need have been. The bitter personal break with Senator Charles Sumner was an even greater blow to the chances of success of the balance of Ulysses Grant's term of office than the loss of Santo Domingo had been. The President and Senator Sumner, each embittered and angry, turned their backs on one another in hostility; standing by, ready to take advantage of their breach, were the many enemies of the noble aspirations for which each had stood.

33

The Unvanquished

★★★★

THE SADDEST chapter in our history is the story of what happened in the South in the period after the Civil War. It is a story of great hopes and greater disappointments. The tragedy of "what might have been" was caused by such injustices against our own people that many historians have not told the whole truth.

The new birth of freedom for the emancipated slave did start to become a reality. Through the economic assistance of the Freedmen's Bureau an effort was made to help that freedom become meaningful. The millions who had been forbidden by the laws of the slave states to learn to read or write now reached out hungrily for education. Teachers were sent from all parts of the country by local Freedmen's Aid Associations that sprang up everywhere. The bureau itself set up some schools, and colleges too, the latter to help train teachers.

The ultimate measure of political freedom was established by the congressional Reconstruction laws. Under these laws, passed over Andrew Johnson's veto, it had been hoped that protection against re-enslavement would be assured by granting to the freedmen the right to vote and the right to hold office. To help in seeing to it that Negroes of the South were afforded equal opportunities and recognized as partners in citizenship, the ex-Confederate states were not to be permitted to send representatives to Congress until they adopted new state constitutions securing these rights.

The Reconstruction laws went into effect almost two years before Ulysses Grant took the oath of office as President. During that period there occurred the initial steps of calling conventions of delegates elected by all the people, Negro and white, except for certain secessionist leaders. These conventions met to write and vote upon wholly new state constitutions so that they could be presented for congressional approval: the first step in genuine, thoroughgoing Reconstruction. Former slaves, as well as Negroes who had been free before the war, met with loyal whites in these state conventions and drew up governmental charters that were later admitted to be among the best that the South had ever seen. Among the new types of constitutional provision for the government of the Southern states was the establishment of free universal public education, something we think of today as an essential part of the American way of life, which many of the slave states never had before. By the time the Grant family entered the White House, all but three of the ex-Rebel states had been accepted by Congress as properly reconstructed.

Unfortunately, however, there had begun during Johnson's Presidency, and grown unchecked, a treasonable conspiracy by what was to become an underground "Secret Army" whose object was to preserve white supremacy. This group began functioning during the Black Code days, when the Johnson-created state governments were already doing business in the old style. It expanded and grew more violent and active when the new democratic state governments were formed. The leaders of this Secret Army, called the Ku Klux Klan, were plantation owners, former slave traders, and Confederate officers. They knew that the cause of secession and slavery was lost. But they felt that they could maintain, or regain, political power by violence, by trickery, and by intimidation.

Their object was as detestable as their methods were lawless: it was to frighten or kill the Negroes and loyal whites who had begun to participate in the new biracial governments and to drive out or destroy the new settlers from the North who had come, for the most part, to educate the freedmen and to invest in and to help rebuild the South that had been ravaged and devastated by war. It must be remembered that at that time there was much of the same kind of race prejudice in the North as there was in the South, and so the objectives of the Ku Klux Klan, while unacceptable to many who felt the whole meaning of the war would be lost if the Klan won, were not as horrifying then as they seem in our eyes today.

As to Ulysses Grant, the effect on his Administration was catastrophic. He was called upon to meet conditions in the South for which there were no actual parallels or precedents and for the existence of which he was in no way to blame. On the contrary: when he returned from his 1865 tour of the postwar South, he had correctly estimated that what the people needed during a period of readjustment of race relationships was full military rule and occupation. The conflict between Johnson and Congress prevented this interlude during which the defeated could begin to rebuild and accept the new economic and social relationships with their former slaves that true emancipation called for, based, as Grant himself put it, on the equal rights which were originally asserted in the Declaration of Independence.

As President, Grant was angered and troubled by the new conditions, but could never formulate a policy adequate to deal with them. The hazards and fortunes of war, the bravery or even the trickery of an enemy on the field, he had the genius to understand and cope with. The hidden enemy, the conspirator, the subversive white coward, who struck at night and disappeared—this was a foe that was difficult to defeat with civilian measures. The reason for Grant's failure was primarily that he was now head of a civilian government, operating under a Constitution that required due process of law in fighting crime. The crime of the Secret Army was guerrilla warfare against established government, and the civilian law enforcement machinery of those days was simply not strong enough to fight it. Even when a criminal was arrested, for example, and his guilt proved, the Constitution's requirement of a jury from the area where the crime took place would result in the presence on the jury of at least a few of those whose sympathy with the criminals was so strong that they would not convict.

Grant's position at the time is often misunderstood, and he has been criticized for the failure of Reconstruction. This criticism is justified to only a limited extent. In the first place, he never forgot his feelings of brotherhood and compassion and magnanimity for the defeated. Those sentiments would perhaps have resulted in fairer treatment of former slaves had the ex-Rebels not been incited otherwise by Johnson. Grant's generosity guided him in the leadership he showed early in his first term of office in completing the reconstruction of Virginia, Mississippi, and Texas. The congressional procedure had stalled here because the people, in referendum, had rejected the constitutions drawn up by the conventions, because of clauses excluding many former Rebels from participating in the governments. The President, speaking in the "confident hope and belief" that the people of these states were "now ready to cooperate with the national Government" suggested that the constitutions be submitted separately, so that the too-strict clauses could be voted upon apart from the rest; he thus cleared the way for the completion of Reconstruction but ultimately, also, for its end.

Grant was ready to be firm and vigorous when he thought his magnanimity had been abused and his trust betrayed. In 1870 he sent a special message to Congress in which he declared that "the free exercise of the franchise has by violence and intimidation been denied to citizens in several of the states lately in rebellion." With this message, asking for new laws, he sent a detailed report of over five thousand cases of Klan floggings, lynchings, and similar outrages. These atrocities all had the same purpose, the elimination of those who could not be beaten at the polls by fair means.

Laws were passed in response to Grant's requests, but what was done under those laws was "too little and too late." One by one the former Confederate states were recaptured by the ex-Rebels and their democratic governments overthrown or displaced. As soon as the political machinery fell into the hands of the "Redeemers," or Bourbons, as the respectable people for whom the Klan was acting were called, they took steps to insure that never again would they be faced with the possibility of biracial government. With the control of the county seats, the state police, and the electoral commissions in their hands, the Bourbons could now do more easily what had been previously accomplished by bloody violence.

Then and later the excuse was given that Negroes and their white partners in the government in the Southern states were "corrupt" and "ignorant." Men always fear the judgment of history and invent excuses for their criminal behavior. Actually there was no more corruption or ignorance in the Southern states in the 70s than in the 50s or the 80s, or than in the rest of the country at any time during the great waves of immigration when big city "bosses" could control or influence the votes of large groups of new citizens and thereby line their own pockets. Many of these big-city political cheats were exposed or jailed; interestingly enough, history does not record any Negro leader of the Reconstruction era who was proved to have wrongfully enriched himself. Some of the migrants, the people of the North and West who settled in the South, were corrupt; a point that is often overlooked is that the activities of the Klan, and the open hostility of many communities to any new settlers who treated the Negroes as human beings, drove out many of the most able and honorable new settlers.

There is no evidence at all that the Negroes in Southern state governments had, on the average, less ability or judgment than their successors or predecessors. The most outstanding characteristic of these people was their hunger and thirst for education; those who were to accuse them of "ignorance" were themselves among the masked mobs who burned down the little schoolhouses where courageous teachers came to satisfy that desire. The Negroes who were sent to Congress worked hard and voted wisely, and it has been conceded by their contemporaries that any race would be proud of them.

Another aspect of Grant's personality that made it hard for him to handle the Reconstruction problems was an insufficient appreciation of the importance of the President's leadership role in our form of government. On becoming President, he said, with all sincerity: "I have no policy to enforce against the will of the people," but in applying this he fell too far behind the people. The citizens of the North and West were themselves, in large measure, infused with race prejudice; many were willing to believe what the white-supremacist-edited Southern papers wrote about the Reconstruction governments. The continuing guerrilla warfare of the Klan and the Redshirts and similar groups achieved its purpose in spreading a mood of retreat among a war-weary people that had responded eagerly to Grant's inaugural words, "Let us have peace."

Grant himself came to reflect these feelings instead of trying to dispel them. Late in his administration, in response to an appeal for help from a state government threatened with insurrection, he declared: "The people are beginning to tire of these annual autumnal outbreaks of violence in the South," and he refused to send the troops that were requested. By the time of the 1876 elections, at the end of his second term, there were only three states in which the Reconstruction governments had not been displaced or overthrown by the Secret Army of the Ku Klux Klan, or its respectable public client, the group known as the Redeemers.

34

Some Constructive Achievements

★★★★

An outstanding aspect of the Grant Administrations was the soldier-President's willingness to search for peaceful solutions to international difficulties. In this effort he was aided and guided by Hamilton Fish of New York, the man he had chosen to be Secretary of State after Elihu Washburne's brief honorary tenure in the post. Whatever the credit that may be due Fish, the basic decisions were Grant's and the choice of Fish as Secretary was his.

The principal problems facing the Grant Administration in the field of foreign affairs were relations with Spain and with Great Britain. Problems with the British went back to the very beginning of the Civil War; difficulties with Spain were produced by a revolt in Cuba, one of the few remaining Spanish colonies in this hemisphere. The new Cuban rebellion flared up just a month before Grant's election. Because of its closeness to our territory, it naturally provided an arena where guerrilla warfare and a fight for freedom would attract the sympathetic attention of the American people. These feelings were played upon and multiplied by the propaganda of exile Cuban groups in New York, the selfish interests they created by giving out "bonds" of the rebel government, and the belligerent cries of a sensational press which beat the drums for some form of intervention—all provided a backdrop of wild exaggerations and inflated casualty lists.

Rawlins, as Grant's Secretary of War, was carried away by sympathy for the insurgents and urged intervention by means of granting recognition. Fish, quiet, resolute, and cautious, urged restraint. He pointed out—and Senator Sumner backed him—that the revolt had not attained the proportions that would justify recognition under the principles of international law. Colorful Dan Sickles, one-legged former Union general, was sent to Spain as ambassador, with instructions to try to negotiate for a money payment to Spain for Cuban independence. The Spanish Government, in financial difficulties, came close to accepting, and then declined the offer for reasons of internal politics. Nevertheless, after Rawlins's death, early in Grant's Administration, Fish was able to prevail upon Grant to accept and apply the principles of international law which required nonintervention.

That very principle was the more easy to accept because it was at the bottom of our difficulties with the British. The first of a series of grievances which aroused great hostility between the two countries, and even provoked demands for the annexation of Canada, was the too early recognition by the British of the "belligerency" of the Confederates. Our complaint was that this act, which conferred on the Rebel group the right to buy arms abroad, was premature under accepted standards. Afterwards British colonies such as Bermuda and the Bahamas were outposts for the blockade runners of the Confederacy. Worst of all, and most flagrantly in violation of international law, was the fitting out in England's own ports of Confederate cruisers, armed with English guns, that raided our shipping and destroyed a good deal of our commerce.

For a period after the close of the war, relations between Great Britain and the United States were strained, a situation that was not made easier by the raids of Irish nationalists on Canadian border areas from United States points as part of their long struggle to win the freedom of their own land. Further irritation might have caused relations to worsen, and yet the Civil War differences and claims remained unresolved throughout the Johnson Administration.

One step taken by Grant toward a solution was Government acquisition of the claims by American citizens against the British for the losses they had suffered. As Fish, under Grant's direction, pressed the American position, the British came to recognize, with troubles arising in Europe, that their own interests required them to recognize and admit that in allowing their ports to be used by expeditions in aid of a rebellion they had violated international law.

The American demands for reparation were called the Alabama claims, so named for the chief Confederate commerce destroyer, built in a British dockyard. The *Alabama* herself had finally been beaten and sunk in 1864 in a fair fight with the U.S.S. *Kearsarge* in the English Channel, in the presence of English spectators who lined the coast to see the show.

After intensive but quiet negotiations the two governments appointed commissioners who met at Washington and worked out the terms of a treaty, named for the city where it was made. It provided an important precedent for the settlement of major international disputes, a pioneering effort to achieve a world ruled by law and order. Five arbitrators, one named by each of five nations, were to meet at Geneva and pass upon the justice of the United States' claims. They were appointed and met for many months and came back with a verdict that Great Britain had been in the wrong and awarded the United States $15,500,000 in damages.

The great triumph for Grant was the establishment of the principle of arbitration—that is, peaceful, neutral decision-making—as a method of disposing of international disagreements. Other important questions were decided by the Treaty of Washington, which lay the foundation for the long and close cooperation between the United States and Great Britain. A commission was established to decide the extent of United States fishing rights in Canadian waters. The German Kaiser, as a neutral head of state, was entrusted with making the decision on a troublesome major boundary question in the Northwest. This left us, said Grant to Congress, "for the first time in the history of the United States as a nation without a question of disputed boundary between our territory and the possessions of Great Britain on this continent."

In an important aspect of internal governmental reform, Grant was a pioneer. We are accustomed now to the appointment of men to most governmental positions on the basis of civil service examinations. Few remember that Grant was the first President to emphasize the need for laws providing for appointment on the basis of merit and not on influence. Lincoln and Johnson, like every President since Andrew Jackson, had accepted the "spoils" system as an ordinary part of running the Government. "To the victor belongs the spoils" meant that a new President would be pressed to fill every job, even the lowest clerkships, from the ranks of the victorious party. Nothing had been done about this evil, which became more pernicious as the Government and its functions expanded, until Senator Charles Sumner introduced a bill in 1864 to establish the merit system. This was treated lightly at the time as another of Sumner's theoretical moral ideas.

Grant's practical experiences as President influenced him to pick up Sumner's idea and push for its adoption. "There is no man in the country," he told a friend later, "so anxious for civil service reform as the President of the United States. He is the one person most interested. Patronage is the bane of the Presidential office. A large share of the vexations and cares of the executive come from patronage. He is necessarily a civil service reformer because he wants peace of mind."

In his second annual message, Grant denounced the spoils system as an abuse of long standing which he would like to see removed at once. He wanted to make merit the test for appointment as well as for tenure of office. A beginning was made. Under his sponsorship, the first Civil Service Reform bill in our history was passed, one providing for a commission to establish regulations to ascertain the fitness of candidates for office.

Congressmen, however, were reluctant to permit the President to follow through. Later generations have blamed Grant for the failure of immediate civil service reform, but he did all that he could to put it over. Too many senators and congressmen were yet unwilling to give up their privileges. Completion of the reform had to await that further development of public sentiment, which alone can move Congress.

Years later Grant commented dryly: "Civil service reform rests entirely with Congress. If members and senators will give up claiming patronage, that will be a step gained. But there is an immense amount of human nature in members of Congress and it is in human nature to seek power and use it and to help friends."

35

Life at the White House

★★★★

Ever since the day, thirty years before, that young Lys started out for West Point, he had always been on the move. When the Grant family moved into the White House in 1869, it was to be the first time they had really settled down in one place—the one address they were to have for the longest period in their lives. To a husband and wife who were so deeply in love that they were not averse to holding hands in public, even in middle age, and equally devoted to their children, it was a welcome pause. "Privacy" they had lost years before, when the capture of Forts Henry and Donelson made Ulysses a national figure.

Two of the Grant children had already grown up to the point where they were completing their education away from home. Fred, who had been at his father's side during much of the Mississippi Valley campaigning, was now a cadet at West Point. Ulysses, Jr., called "Buck" for the Buckeye state of Ohio, where he was born when Lieutenant Sam was in the far Northwest, was a freshman at Harvard. The active White House children of the 70s were Nellie Grant—fourteen when she moved in—and young Jesse, who had been named for his grandfather.

The President was indulgent and tolerant in every family relationship, and so Grandpa Dent, his father-in-law, a widower now, was allowed to move into the White House as part of the household. He must have irritated, perhaps exasperated, the President at times, as he not only made himself at home but held "court" after a fashion, repeatedly denouncing, to all who would listen, the rights accorded to the freedmen and the lawmakers who sought to protect them from their former masters. Grant never complained. Even if he were not such a gentleman; his feelings for Julia would have restrained him. Old Jesse Grant, however, as a former abolitionist, would not allow the former slaveowner to get off so easily. Jesse lived with Hannah in Covington, Kentucky, where he had become postmaster under Johnson, but he visited the White House often to see his son and grandchildren. He never failed to spar with stubborn old "Colonel" Dent—and held his own.

When the General-in-Chief took off his uniform and entered the White House, it was with the sincere wish and intention to be a civilian leader and not a military commander. On the very first night the family dined at the executive mansion they thought they heard a rhythmic tramp of feet outside the dining room. Holding his napkin in his hand, the President strode over to the door and pulled it open—to find a sentry in uniform marching back and forth.

"How many of you are there around the building?" asked Grant.

Standing at attention the soldier answered, "Two at each entrance, sir, and two on each floor."

"Since when have we had military sentinels posted in the White House?"

"Since the war began, sir."

"Go tell your commander," the President said gently, "that I don't want sentries here. Have the others recalled, too."

Grant tried to behave as he thought a nonmilitary leader should, and now that he was in a civilian position, he was democratic in his ways. He would often saunter about the streets of Washington, stopping to talk to a friend or window-shopping in the business section hear the White House. He enjoyed evening visits outside the official residence, often with Julia and sometimes "stag," without her. He almost always seemed to be carrying a cigar, either one that he was smoking or one that he was about to smoke. He had a genuine dislike for the formality involved in having to send for men in the Government to come to see him, and would often stroll out to see a Cabinet member or senator with whom he wanted to talk. In part, however, this may have been a reflection of his impatience to "get things done"—as when, at the time of a critical debate on the Santo Domingo treaty, Grant went to the Senate anteroom and personally lobbied for its passage.

His daily routine would rarely vary. He was always up at seven and would read the Washington morning newspapers until he heard breakfast announced. Then, if Julia was not down yet—and usually she was not—he would knock at her door.

"Is that you Ulyss?" she would call out.

"Breakfast is ready."

"I will be there in a few minutes, General."

Sometimes he would have to wait a little while longer, and always did so, uncomplainingly. After breakfast he would escort Julia to the sitting room, and then go out, light a cigar, and take a short stroll, walking slowly with his left hand held behind his back, waist high, the cigar held forward in his right. At ten o'clock he would return and go to the Presidential offices to see to the day's business and receive visitors—who usually noted that he listened to all that was said but was silent or noncommittal in his replies. His principal secretaries and staff assistants in the White House were former soldiers, still holding the military rank they had earned on his staff in the war. They were chosen not because they were military men, but because Grant knew and trusted them and had had so few civilian contacts before he became President, except with very wealthy businessmen who had made a point, as leaders of their communities, of entertaining

Ulysses and Julia in their town and country homes after the war.

Washington, arena of bitter personal conflict during Johnson's last years, became a center of a new sort of social life; new in the sense not only that ten years had passed since there had been any social life centered about the White House, but also in that the postwar Washington of the early 70s was a reflection of the new kind of country we were becoming. The changes in our national life and standards came not on account of the Grants, but despite them, and swept them along into the whirl. There was much vulgar ostentation—"showing off"—of the newly rich, the millionaire class the war had developed, which had grown with the postwar industrial and railroad building upsurge. Competition of money and power for social and strategic position dominated the scene. Julia grew to enjoy Washington society and the responsibilities as First Hostess, which she had carried awkwardly at first. Ulysses never could accept social obligations cheerfully and seemed to discharge them, even though without complaint, as though they were a grim duty.

Nellie Grant began life in the White House as a shy young teenager; at her father's inauguration she ran over to him from the platform seat assigned to her and stood by him, holding his hand, until a chair was brought over so she could be near him while he took the oath of office and delivered the inaugural address. As the months passed, however, she quickly grew out of the children's circle at the White House and became leader of a young social set in capital activity. Anti-Administration newspapers were quick to exaggerate and criticize—so much so that one important visitor was pleased and startled to find on firsthand acquaintance that the almost notorious Nellie was just "a very pretty girl of sixteen. Behaves just as well as any other well-bred girl would."

Later, as the 1872 elections approached, criticism of Nellie's social life convinced Julia and Ulysses that they should send her on a trip to Europe with former Secretary of the Navy Adolph Borie and his wife, even though the criticism was more noisy than justified. The Bories were happy to oblige the Grants by escorting Nellie on what they thought would be a quiet and relaxing trip. The Grant name, however, was too glamorous to be overlooked, and Nellie's shining personality added to its luster; she was presented at Queen Victoria's Court and carried herself well through a round of parties and receptions that soon sent the Bories homeward, months before they expected to return.

On the voyage back Nellie met and fell in love with a shipboard acquaintance. He was Algernon Sartoris, a young Englishman, nephew of the world-famous actress Fanny Kemble, whose own connection with the United States had been romantic and tragic. Long before the Civil War, Mrs. Kemble had met and married Pierce Butler, a wealthy slave-owning Philadelphian, who had carried her off to his Georgia plantation to live. It was not to be happily ever after. She had been shocked and dismayed by the realization, at first hand, of the unhappy lot of the slaves, and her marriage was wrecked. Years later, but before the Civil War ended, her diary was published and became a significant factor in opening European eyes to the brutality and degradation of humanity that was concealed behind the Rebel war slogans about the plantation "way of life."

Nellie had told her parents about Algie Sartoris before he came to call at the executive mansion. They were as reluctant as any parents would be in the circumstances to give their consent. Algie had dinner at the White House and afterwards withdrew with the President for a cigar in the billiard room. He trembled, hesitated, fidgeted and coughed—and hoped that Grant would make his task easier, but the grim-lipped President did not say a word. Finally, feeling as though he were about to sink through the floor, he stammered, "Mr. President, I want to marry your daughter."

By then Julia and Ulysses had agreed reluctantly that they could not withhold their consent, when and if they should be asked. In due course there followed one of the notable White House weddings of our history, with the Capitol decked in flowers for the occasion, and the diplomatic corps in full regalia. The Marine Band played softly, and the gifts brought by the noted guests were as sumptuous as the clothes they wore. After the ceremony it was noted that Grant was missing. He was found alone, in Nellie's room, sobbing softly at the departure of his only daughter.

Jesse, who had begun living at the White House at age eleven, had unusual childhood memories, one of the first being a recollection of the dim, shadowy interior of the boxcar in which he and his mother had escaped from Holly Springs, Mississippi, just before Rebel raiders swept the town during the early Vicksburg campaign. Jesse was a typical Tom Sawyerish, freckle-faced small boy, in good health and usually in high spirits. As such he created no more and no less of a problem in the President's house than would any nineteenth-century boy of his type. Many boys from the neighborhood gathered to play on the White House grounds in fair weather and in its roomy basement in foul.

When his playmates were not around, Jesse could and did spend many hours, contented and carefree, in the White House stables, which were well populated. As Jesse said, "Father never sold a horse in his life." Grant did not mount the saddle any more, but he did take great pleasure in an afternoon airing in one of the carriages behind a pair of the fine horses in which he delighted.

One story of Jesse's life in the White House was later told by Jesse himself when he was past seventy. His grandfather Grant had promised, when the boy was nine, to present him with an impressive old gold watch that he sported; this was meant as an incentive to young Jesse's scholastic work, which was then lagging. Later on old Jesse put off

BETTMANN ARCHIVE

President Grant enjoys a brisk carriage ride, driving his horse, Dexter.

keeping his promise and the boy was miserable. When the following Christmas approached, he asked his father if he could write to Grandfather at Covington to remind him about the watch.

"I would not write," said the President; "wait until you see him again."

That day Grant left the White House and walked over to a nearby jeweler's and purchased a small gold watch. He brought the watch home before dinner that evening and showed it to Julia and Nellie, pledging them to secrecy. He explained that it was to be a Christmas gift to Jesse.

That same night, while the family was at dinner, the father drew the watch from his pocket and handed it to Jesse.

"Here is your watch, Jesse."

"Why, Ulyss!" Julia exclaimed, "You said that was to be his Christmas present."

Grant turned to Jesse with a broad, warm grin.

"Jesse doesn't want to wait until Christmas, and neither do I," he said.

The family spent many happy hours together at a cottage that Ulysses and Julia bought at the New Jersey summer resort of Long Branch, first of the summer White Houses. Ulysses enjoyed the relaxed atmosphere of his summer home more than life in the White House, and when he was not at Long Branch to escape the humid days and depressing nights of the Washington summer, he traveled through the country. He was never more at ease than at his retreat at the Jersey shore.

As his Administration went on, partisan attacks multiplied, many without justification, many based on genuine grievances at his shortcomings. Among the less warranted of the attacks was the accusation of spending too much time at Long Branch. Toward the end of his second term a hostile House of Representatives passed an impertinent resolution, asking information on the number of Presidential duties that had been performed away from Washington. With justice the President answered that it was not only possible for him to work away from the White House, but that he had done much while away; to his answer he appended an impressive list of absences by prior Presidents from the nation's capital.

36

Second Term

★★★★

As THE FIRST Grant term of office came to a close in 1872 there was a rising tide of disaffection in the ranks of his own party and a chorus of bitter hostility from the "outs." The developing opposition had begun early in his first term, when many were displeased to find that the President was not the same kind of genius at the art of statesmanship that he had been at the task of leading the country to victory in civil war. The greater the expectation, the greater the disappointment: this rule of human nature explains an intolerance of errors committed by Ulysses Grant that might have been overlooked in a lesser man.

The most outstanding defection from his own party ranks was that of the great Senator Charles Sumner, whose break with the Administration over the Santo Domingo policy became the more irreparable because of Grant's own stubborn determination, which magnified the issue into an importance which it never deserved. Others deserted him because of changing personal views on the great issues of Reconstruction, and their latent racial prejudices having come to the fore, they opposed even such ineffectual and sporadic attempts as Grant had led to enforce the civil rights laws of that period. Still others, for a variety of reasons, some personal and selfish, some sincere, joined the defectors in what was called a "Liberal Republican" movement to unseat Grant. Some of these had been repelled because of a growing dependence by the President on the machine politicians in his party's congressional delegation, to whom he had turned when he needed assistance for his legislative program. The death of Secretary of War Rawlins, who was more of a general adviser than Cabinet member, deprived the President of an able and confidential counselor who might have protected him from some of the pitfalls of practical politics.

The opponents joined a political coalition and nominated one-time crusading and abolitionist newspaper editor Horace Greeley to lead the ticket. The main issue before the country was, pretty much, whether the Presidency of Grant should be approved—and it was, by a large margin. Grant, who had declined to campaign actively, partly because of his continuing chronic shyness, took great satisfaction in the result. He had been more hurt than he had admitted by the malignant criticism that mounted during his first term and showed his feelings in his second inaugural address: "I have been the subject of abuse and slander, scarcely ever equalled in political history, which today I feel that I can afford to disregard, in view of your verdict, which I gratefully accept as my vindication."

Although the Grant family were all in good spirits on the second Inaugural Day, the weather was unpropitious. The wind was at gale force and the temperature far below freezing. The stormy weather was an accurate omen of difficult days to come. The rule has been that a President's second term of office is less happy than his first, and Grant was particularly miserable during his.

Even before the technical beginning of the new term of office, the Washington headlines had been dominated by the exposure of the so-called Credit Mobilier scandal. What is rarely remembered now, although the scandal is always mentioned as a leading factor in what has come to be called "Grantism," is that the events that were uncovered in the investigation of this scheme of railroad promoters to influence congressmen by easy stock profits took place long *before*

Grant had become President. Likewise without any direct or even indirect personal responsibility, Grant's name was besmirched on the eve of the second inaugural by a "Salary Grab" law. This law which distributed "back pay" for an increase in congressional salary voted at the end of the term, was attached as a rider to an essential appropriation act, and Grant was forced to sign it.

More serious in its effects on the country than these minor scandals was the sudden and unexpected onset of an economic crisis which erupted within five months after the second term began and led to a depressed economy that lasted for the balance of the term. America had experienced business slumps in 1837 and 1857, before it had really completed its transformation from an eastern coastal strip of agricultural ex-colonies to an industrial power. The tremendous factory expansion of the Civil War and immediate postwar period was a change unlike any that had gone before, and with it came boom times, speculation, and the multiple growth of new fortunes. The center and fulcrum of the postwar expansion was the fanning out of a railroad network across the nation. The growth of the new roads, their management, and the business of selling their securities was totally unregulated, as was true of practically all business. As Gould and Fisk had shown with the Erie, one could say that the railroads "regulated" many state governments and dominated many aspects of the national Government. The Credit Mobilier scandal was but the first notable example of this extraordinary power.

As a result of the postwar period of profit, prosperity, and perpetual optimism, a point had been reached by the summer of 1873 where too much had been invested in railroad stocks of doubtful value, and the roads had expanded beyond the commercial and transportation needs of the fast-growing nation. The aftermath of a cycle of European wars caused bank failures in Vienna, Berlin, Paris, and London, and cautious businessmen and financiers in New York began

BETTMANN ARCHIVE

President Ulysses S. Grant, Vice-President Wilson and the cabinet prepare to leave for the capitol for the second inauguration, 1869.

to hoard gold. Early in September several banking houses and one new railroad went into bankruptcy.

The most prominent Wall Street banker of the day was Jay Cooke, a man whose firm had been heavily involved in railroad stock speculation. Cooke had cultivated Grant's friendship long before the general himself had realized that he was going to be the next President. Cooke had been a heavy contributor and efficient fundraiser for the party in 1868 and 1872. Simply because he had come to be a friend of the family, Ulysses and young Jesse were spending the night of September 17, 1873 at Cooke's Pennsylvania country home. Julia and her husband had chosen a boarding school in the neighborhood for Jesse to attend; while they were there, Cooke gave Jesse a fishing rod to help him get used to the idea of living away from home. Urgent messages started to come in for the white-bearded banker, but, being a perfect host, he did not breathe a word that would spoil the visit of his noted house guests.

Back in Washington the next day, the President kept his usual calm with difficulty as a messenger came in with the news that Jay Cooke and Company had failed: it had closed its doors because it was unable to meet its Wall Street obligations. With remarkable speed the flimsy structure of national prosperity seemed to collapse. In a matter of days banks began to close all over the country. The stock exchange suspended operations. Far and wide across the land industrial and commercial paralysis began to spread. The first major depression of the modern industrial era had begun. There was at hand neither Government know-how nor Government controls to help fight the disaster or influence its course.

Grant moved quickly to do what he could. Within three days after Cooke's downfall, the President traveled to New York with his Secretary of the Treasury and let it be known that he was available for consultation with the business community. He listened carefully, in a suite at a lower Fifth Avenue hotel, as throngs of bankers, brokers, capitalists, merchants, manufacturers, and railroad men called upon him.

They agreed in demanding that the Government come to their rescue, but not on the method to be used. Many thought at first that inflation of the currency—the addition of greenbacks to the circulation of money—would be the cure-all. Grant stood fast against such a measure.

The worst of the panic passed, the stock exchange reopened, but for the common people the "hard times" persisted. By the end of 1873 over five thousand businesses, capitalized at a total of over a quarter of a billion dollars, closed their doors and threw their workers out of jobs. During this period the downward spiral of business and trade was slowed, although not checked, by the President's decision to permit the Secretary of the Treasury to purchase Government bonds with national banknotes, the result of the purchases being to put money into circulation. Congressman James A. Garfield, who was later to be President himself, had been among those who had begun to lose faith in Grant's abilities as a civilian leader. However, after a White House visit during this troubled period, he remarked that Grant had shown that he had given serious and constructive consideration to the nation's financial difficulties.

Early in 1874 one of the most dramatic and striking incidents of Grant's second term occurred. The widespread business troubles and general hardship that followed the onset of the depression dominated the Congress that met in December. Its members came forward with a large number and wide variety of schemes for alleviating business difficulties by tampering with the currency. The regulation of business practices, control of security dealings, or promotion of public works programs were far beyond history's horizon at the time. The congressmen united on a bill to provide for an inflationary increase in the amount of money in circulation, and the bill was passed by good majorities and sent to the President. Public sentiment, molded by the pressure to "do something," was heavily weighted in favor of the bill and the President was faced with a difficult decision.

"I never was so pressed in my life to do anything as to sign that bill—never," he said to a friend later on. "It was represented to me that the veto would destroy the Republican Party in the West; that the West and South would combine and take the country, and agree on some even worse plan of finance." Actually, Grant confessed, he even went so far as to make an effort to compose a message to Congress, giving reasons for signing the bill. When he finished writing it and read it over, he was so dissatisfied that he threw it aside and resolved to do what he believed was right and vetoed the bill. While he received much credit then and later for his courage in exercising the veto, that was not reflected in the 1874 congressional elections, which were a stinging defeat for his party. The continuing hard times took their toll and put his Administration at the mercy of an opposition House of Representatives for its last two years.

That period was dominated by the embarrassment of two scandals that involved Grant's own appointees. Even his bitterest enemies did not claim that Grant was personally involved in these affairs. However, the fight for factional advantage within his own party and the opportunity presented to the opposition for noisy propaganda combined to stain Grant's name and mark his Administration as "scandal-ridden." It may be that what has distinguished Grant's Presidency from those of many of his successors was not that there were more abuses in public office during his time but rather that more abuses and instances of corrupt practices were exposed.

It takes two to make a bribe a crime. The man or organization that buys a favor from a Government official is as guilty as the man who sells his integrity and abuses his trust and betrays his chief. One sad case was that of his Secretary of War, who had control of the appointment of trading officials at Indian posts, and whose wife enriched herself by a percentage of the income that was gained by these officials. The scandal of largest scope, however, and the one that hurt Ulysses Grant the most, was the case of the so-called Whisky Ring.

To pay for the enormous costs of the Civil War and the interest on the war debt, a new scale of high taxes had been imposed on the distilling of whisky, which had been so cheap and plentiful before. Unscrupulous businessmen saw a chance to increase their already large profits in this trade by bribing the Government inspectors who were supposed to measure and certify their output in order to determine how much tax was to be paid. Higher officials were in on the scheme, in order to permit it to go on, especially in the scale and quantity involved.

The wide investigation that exposed and smashed the "ring" was started by Grant's own Secretary of the Treasury. During the course of the investigation, charges were made that one of Grant's own White House secretaries had connived with the conspirators. When these accusations came to Grant's knowledge, he wrote a note to the investigators saying, "Let no guilty man escape."

The man accused was General Orville Babcock. He had long been a faithful friend and close co-worker of Grant's; it was he who had delivered Grant's last letter to Lee before the meeting at Appomattox. Babcock was the man who had said, after the war, that it would be a misfortune for Grant if he were to enter civilian politics. Babcock came to trial late in the course of the investigation. The President, with unflagging loyalty but doubtful wisdom, insisted on testifying as a character witness in favor of his aide; he knew nothing of the facts of the case, he said, but declared that he had "always had great confidence in his integrity and efficiency." The evidence against Babcock was inconclusive, and perhaps Grant's character testimony balanced the scales. General Babcock was acquitted by the jury, but a shadow always hung over his name.

37

Who Won in 1876— and Who Lost

★★★★

IT WAS A depression year, the third year of the worst business crisis America had ever suffered. In the industrial Northeast both employed and unemployed workers were restless and discontented. In the Midwest and the Far West dissatisfied farmers, who had difficulty making ends meet as prices fell, combined with mining interests to put forward new schemes based on the use of silver as currency. In the South eight of the former eleven Confederate states were under the control of the Redeemer groups—men who had used guerrilla warfare and other techniques of force or fraud to gain power so that they could establish domination instead of partnership as the basis of race relations. In the remaining three—South Carolina, Louisiana, and Florida—the Reconstruction governments were weakened by division among their leaders; the Secret Army groups edged closer to seizure of power. The survival of these last three remaining biracial governments depended upon skillful and bold national leadership. The President would have to combat a rising tide of Northern opinion that was tiring of the problem. The ideals of the Declaration of Independence that had been given genuine content in the Constitution by the Fourteenth and Fifteenth amendments were in danger again.

A President willing to lead might have checked the

trend toward lawless disregard of the Constitution. The Southern-born historian Woodrow Wilson admitted that replacement of biracial state governments by white dictatorships was brought about by "keeping the Negroes away from the polls by every form of intimidation, by forcible interference with their rights when necessary, by every expedient, whether of law or of subtle management, that promised them mastery."

Grant had tried his best, in his own way, to provide leadership in the enforcement of the laws designed to prevent such results. He had failed. He lacked the gift for leading public opinion and failed to understand how to use the moral authority of his office to combat the prejudice or apathy—the "What do I care?" attitude—that had paralyzed the rest of the nation. Besides, the rising hostility during the last years of his Presidency had almost overwhelmed him. Political friends became enemies; personal friends had used or attempted to use their connection with him solely to advance their own private interests. The public had come to think badly of him and he felt keenly the seeming loss of that wide personal popularity that had made his election inevitable eight years before.

Some of his Republican followers thought that a third term would give him an opportunity to help them retain party control and regain the losses he had suffered. Grant, however, firmly put an end to such talk by writing to a state party convention that he was not and would not be a candidate for a second renomination. He was tired of the endless controversy and sense of frustration and wanted to retire. When he announced that he would not run he did so against Julia's wishes, for she had come to like life in the White House and all that it meant.

The President's withdrawal led to an open convention for the first time in the Republican Party since 1860. The nomination was finally won by Governor Rutherford B. Hayes of Ohio, a "dark horse." The Democrats, scenting a chance for their first victory in twenty years, nominated a popular candidate, Governor Tilden of New York. He was a reformer who had won fame by his exposure and prosecution of corrupt upstate and downstate New York politicians who had stolen state and city funds greater in amount, probably, than had been wrongfully taken in all the Southern states put together. Since factions hostile to the President had united behind the Hayes nomination, Grant practically ceased to be the leader of his own party; nevertheless he spoke and campaigned for the nominee.

Both parties watched the telegraph wires anxiously on November 7, 1876. Never had there been such a close and exciting election. Because of the eight Southern states in which Negroes had been kept from the polls in large numbers—the beginning of the Solid South—plus a number of victories in Northern states, it began to look as if Tilden had won the election. He definitely led in the popular vote, but the outcome of the electoral vote count was uncertain. Most newspapers blared forth the news that the Democrats had won. Grant at a social gathering in Philadelphia scanned the returns that aides brought in to him and said,

"Gentlemen, it looks to me as if Mr. Tilden was elected."

Republican Presidential candidate Hayes likewise thought that he had been defeated, and fearing the Democratic regime would mean consolidation of the Secret Army successes in the South, he confided in a friend, "I don't care for myself; and the party, yes, and the country, too, can stand it, but I do care for the poor colored men of the South."

"What do you mean?" asked the friend.

"The result will be," answered Hayes, "that the Southern people will practically treat the Constitutional amendments as nullities and then the colored man's fate will be worse than when he was in slavery, with a humane master to look after his interests. That is the only reason I regret the news as it is."

As the situation developed it became clear that, with 185 electoral votes necessary to elect, Tilden was certain to receive 184 and Hayes 166. The missing votes were accounted for by Louisiana, Florida, and South Carolina, the combined total of which would have given Hayes the election. A thrill of excitement ran through the nation. Reports began to come in of grave disorders at the South. Secretary of State Fish told of the wrecking of trains, tearing up of telegraph wires, and general disturbances. Only a few months before, there had been a pre-election massacre of innocent Negroes in Hamburg, South Carolina, which Grant had called "cruel, bloodthirsty, wanton and unprovoked." Now Northern Democrats, too, power-hungry and out of office for sixteen years, became restless and talked of violent measures, as they feared the Republican Administration would certify the vote count in Hayes' favor.

Historians have never wholly agreed as to what a fair and honest count of the votes in the disputed states would have shown. The consensus was that despite all the intimidation by "rifle clubs" and other practitioners of threats and violence, South Carolina and Florida did vote for Hayes. The outcome in Louisiana may have been in favor of Tilden by actual count, but conditions in the local election districts had been such that no one can say that the count represented the true sentiment of the eligible voters of the districts. General Sherman, Commander of the United States Army, who had been against Negro suffrage, summarized the unbiased military reports from some of those districts in a letter to Hayes: "It seems more like the history of hell than of civilized and Christian communities. . . . That you would have received at a fair election a large majority in Louisiana, no honest man can question."

Public feeling in the rival camps reached the point where there was talk of two Presidential inaugurations, no matter who should be certified as having won. The Northern Democrats, who numbered among their leaders many anti-

Negro "copperheads" of the stripe that had advocated defeatist policies during the war, began to scheme to inaugurate Tilden in New York City if Hayes should be declared elected.

Grant's finest and strongest qualities came to the fore in this national emergency. Orders were given to be ready to put New York in a state of siege should an attempt at a disloyal inauguration be made. Plans were made to cut off the land approaches to the city and, with the aid of the Navy, to cut off its supplies of food and water. It was recalled that a proslavery mayor of New York had threatened to secede in sympathy with the South at the beginning of the war because of the vast and complex ties of the New York commercial community with the slave-based cotton trade. The South, too, was not neglected in Grant's precautions. The President ordered the regional army post commanders there to "be vigilant with the forces at their command to preserve peace and good order, and to see that the proper and legal boards of canvassers are unmolested in the performance of their duties. . . . No man worthy of the office of President should be willing to hold it if counted in or placed there by fraud."

While Grant was taking every precaution to see that the recount in the doubtful states was fairly and accurately made, supporters of Hayes were not sitting back quietly to await the outcome. Secret meetings were taking place, and confidential letters were being written which were to determine who was to be accepted as the next President of the United States, and at what price.

For some years Northern business interests had been increasingly unhappy about the continued threat to commercial stability and profitable trade that resulted from the turmoil produced by the advance of the Secret Army to power. They had misgivings as to the effects of the sporadic efforts of the national Government to check the uprisings, and began to feel an increasing community of interest with the white leaders of "property and intelligence," as they called them, who would not accept racial equality. The Northern business groups had stepped up their demands for what they called "leniency" toward the white South; what they had in mind we would call "appeasement" today. One recent historian has summed it up: "Where economic interests jibed . . . men of business were men of peace." New Yorkers, Bostonians, Chicagoans, with railroad interests or cotton interests or investment interests, began to feel that there might be some merit in washing the nation's hands of the whole troublesome situation and leaving the South to solve its racial problems on the terms laid down by the unreconstructed, that is, the racist whites.

This growing mood of appeasement was seized upon by a group of crafty personal supporters of Hayes, who began to work toward securing an attitude of neutrality on the part of the Democratic congressmen from the South. If the Southern and Northern Democrats had remained united, troublesome obstacles would have been placed in the way of declaring Hayes elected, since the House of Representatives had fallen into the hands of the opposition in the 1874 elections. No "deal" could be made with the Northern Democrats and none was wanted. But there was an area of common interest which made it possible for the Hayes supporters to come to terms with the Deep South opposition congressmen and win their acquiescence to the Republican candidate's victory.

Not being associated with the faction in the party that had remained loyal to Grant and his policy of law enforcement, these Hayes Republicans had no objections on the grounds of moral principle to yielding to the white South on the first condition of any settlement: abandonment of the policy of enforcing by Federal action the war-born Constitutional amendments guaranteeing civil rights and the right to vote. That these constitutional guarantees had been passed in recognition, among other things, of the contribution of the Negro soldiers to Union victory meant little or nothing to these men. True, the Southerners had hopes that such abandonment would follow Tilden's installation in office, and that in addition they would be awarded the usual crop of Federal jobs that go to a victorious national party; but that, too, could be arranged by Hayes supporters, and so the door was opened to further bargaining.

The very nature of the two parties as they were then formed made such bargaining a practical possibility. The Northern Democrats who would have been foremost in the national administration and would have dominated Congress under Tilden included many heirs of the old Jacksonian Democrats who opposed "special interests," favored low tariffs, and believed that Federal subsidies for railroads, canals, river and harbor dredging, and other internal improvements were a waste of taxpayers' money. The Southern Democrats, on the other hand, included men of the old-time Whig Party that had fallen apart on the slavery issue on the eve of the Civil War. These men, with their conservative and business-minded philosophy, who had always opposed the Jacksonians before the war, were much closer to the outlook of Hayes and his supporters than to the Northern Democrats. They resented the growth of Northern railroads with Government aid during the war, only because it had not been matched after the war by similar development in the South. They felt that their business interests would prosper and expand if a Southern-route transcontinental railroad were to be built.

This fitted in exactly with the hopes and intentions of a group of railroad lobbyists who had become highly skilled at developing alliances within both parties, and who controlled the votes of a number of congressmen. These men had concluded that their expansionist plans would be aided if a Republican Administration were to be installed with Southern cooperation and without further troublesome agitation of the questions of human rights that had so often preoccupied the Congress and the Presidency in the immediate past.

The bargain was developed over a period of many weeks. Too many people were involved for it to be a complete secret, but none of its terms were formal and few were even put clearly into words. However, the *Enquirer*, a shrewd and observant Cincinnati newspaper, whose reporters may have gotten off-the-record statements from the bargainers, summed it up very well:

> As an inducement to secure the votes in the House to complete the election of Hayes, the guarantees to the South are: first, one or two cabinet places; second, the control of their own state governments; third, a guaranteed policy on the part of the Republicans of liberal appropriations for Southern internal improvements; fourth, the passage of the Texas Pacific Railroad bill.

Such was the path to power of the men who had attacked the Grant Administration as being "corrupt," the so-called Liberal Republicans of that period. The bitterly disputed election was settled without the need to resort to force. Grant and his family quietly left the White House, which was politely turned over to Hayes at a dinner party, while Northern Democrats fumed and raged. But the real victims were those who had been cheated out of much more than mere temporary office. The Americans who had been short-changed in the bargaining, and who were to be driven back from the verge of freedom to a state of subjection and repression, were the Negroes in the South.

38

Around the World

"WE'RE GOING, Jesse. That's settled," the President said, his face lighting up for the first time in months, when his youngest son came home from college for Christmas in 1876. "We start as soon as possible after my successor is installed. We will take whatever money there is and we will go as far and stay as long as it lasts."

The tanner's son had enjoyed most his overnight trips with horse and carriage; growing up, he had dreamed of life as a river boatman; as a youth, he consoled himself on the way to West Point with the sheer pleasure of the journey itself. Ulysses Grant had always hoped to see the world, and when he left the White House he had his chance.

Julia, Ulysses, and Jesse sailed from Philadelphia in mid-May. Beyond seeing Nellie in England, they had no particular plans except to travel as long as their savings lasted. Between the day he left the executive mansion in March and the day they sailed, Grant found that he was not going to slip into discredited obscurity. The steam whistles, salutes, and flags that followed their ship down the river were the culmination of popular manifestation and friendly editorials from critics, only recently hostile, that had followed the end of his term and departure from Washington. "Why," he said, brightening up after suffering sniping and hostility for months, "it is just as it was immediately after the war!" And Julia, remembering how she had felt for him during that bitter period when blame for all the nation's ills had been heaped on her husband, had whispered to Jesse: "They understand now and are sorry."

Even the new Administration, which had seemed to want to dissociate itself from Grant's policies and offend him in its appointments—policies and appointments that were the fruit of the deal that had put it in power—could not ignore the public reaction. After his ship sailed a note was sent abroad to all United States diplomats, stressing "the enthusiastic manifestation of popular regard and esteem for General Grant shown by the people of all parts of the country that he has visited since his retirement from official life" and asking them to aid in making his journey pleasant.

The note was unnecessary. England, where they first landed, was to set the pattern for a type of reception that no American or, indeed, no one, had ever received consistently and repeatedly and spontaneously in every quarter of the globe. Kings, emperors, viceroys, were to call on him. Little girls in mission schools in India and Siam were to greet him by singing "John Brown's Body." The journey that had been expected to be, at most, for six months was to last twenty-eight and extend to every continent except newly settled Australia.

While the Lord Chamberlain and the royal Court of Queen Victoria were splitting hairs and debating over what rank, if any, should be given to a mere ex-President, the common people of England were taking the matter into their own hands. When Grant and his family landed at Liverpool, ten thousand English workers pushed through the custom house to give their unofficial welcome. His trip to London was like a triumphal procession. The explanation was not difficult to seek.

Europe of the 1870s reigned over the world's still growing group of colonial empires and was itself a continent of monarchies and autocracies; England was a nation of deeply divided social classes, seemingly permanently stratified. The presence of this former President who had been born a tanner's son in a two-room cottage was a personification of what they had read about but had not seen: a plain man of humble background who could rise to lead a nation solely because of the merits of his character and ability.

Besides this, the working people had sympathized with the Union in its struggle to survive. They knew that their high society and their mill owners were on the side of slavery; they had themselves suffered through the unemployment that resulted from the blockade of the cotton ports and done so uncomplainingly because they had felt that human freedom was worth the price. They had met during the war in mass meetings to pass resolutions expressing "regret that any of our countrymen should have displayed a feeling of sympathy with those in America who are fighting to establish an oligarchical government on the basis of the enslavement of a weak and defenseless race."

Typical of the receptions accorded the family by the manufacturing and mining districts of England was that of the Newcastle region. The houses and shops were decorated with flags and the church bells were ringing. Along the banks of the River Tyne were lined 150,000 people, mostly workmen, many carrying signs inscribed "Welcome General Grant" and "Let Us Have Peace"—the last words of his address of acceptance of the Presidential nomination. The chief speaker who addressed the Newcastle mass meeting said in recalling the people's feeling about the Civil War:

"Never was there a war in which English armies were not employed that went so directly to the popular feeling. This was not merely because their kinsmen were in mortal combat, but because it was a battle for great principles. It was not a war for conquest, for selfish aggrandizement, or for the propping up of a tottering throne; but it involved the great question of freedom, of the rights of man, and the dignity and honor of labor."

In his response Grant said simply: "I am a man of peace. I have always advocated peace. I never willingly, although

I have gone through two wars, advocated war." The people cheered. The local papers said next day: "Looking like an ordinary Tyneside skipper, open-browed, firm-faced, bluff, honest, and unassuming, everybody at once settled in his own mind that the General would do."

A man of peace he proved himself wherever he went. Repeatedly he was offered a review of troops to mark his arrival and almost invariably he firmly declined. "I never again want to see a military parade," he said.

In his travels he showed that he liked people more than scenery, and the common people best of all. At every town and village, as soon as the party stopped for the night, he wanted to stroll out and watch the crowds returning from work, or in their shops or at play or at festival. James Russell Lowell, who was United States Ambassador to Spain, wrote that "he likes best to escape and wander about the streets. After being here two days I think he knows Madrid better than I."

This interest in people everywhere did not mean that Grant was sympathetic to the economic problems of the working man in that period of rapid and uncontrolled industrial growth. The newly rich of America had sought his friendship, and he had responded by identifying himself and the interests of his country with those whose industrial leadership had helped to win the war and had dominated the nation's phenomenal postwar growth. Like most Americans of that day, Grant had little understanding of the economic forces which made his friends' wealth and America's progress dependent on miserly low wages and oppressive working conditions for the millions who had built and who ran the railroads and factories. During 1877 there took place a series of great railroad strikes in response to the reductions of the wage rates imposed during the Hayes Administration. At the very moment when he was touched and pleased by the warm and enthusiastic greetings of the English workingmen, Grant wrote to his brother-in-law, Corbin, that the European papers were "full of the great strike." It was his judgment, he said, without considering the case of the American working man, "that it should have been put down with a strong hand and so summarily as to prevent a like occurrence for a generation." It was.

This was a period in America and in much of Europe when wealth was more appreciated than culture. Good taste was at a low ebb and Grant's was no better than most of his contemporaries. He did not particularly appreciate the art treasures of Europe. The famed Uffizi Gallery and Pitti Palace in Florence bored him, and when he came to the Vatican, where he had been invited to an audience with the Pope, he passed through the wonderful galleries of statuary without lingering. While he was blind to the beauties of art, this much can be said—he did not pretend. In Paris he sneaked off, while Julia was at the Louvre, to go to the office of the New York *Herald* and read the American papers. "I have seen nothing here that would make me want to live in Paris," he said.

One deficiency in his make-up had been gradually overcome during his Presidency and he had ample opportunity in Europe and across the rest of the world to develop and display his new talent. As general he had always been cordial and communicative among his intimates; he feared no enemy; and yet he was terror-stricken when an occasion called for him to speak in public. On his way to the rescue of Chattanooga he faced without flinching the prospect of entering the besieged and starving town and did not complain of his painful leg injury that kept him on crutches. However, he had to stop on the way at Nashville and was there greeted with a long speech of welcome by Andrew Johnson, then military governor of liberated Tennessee. Grant later said of this meeting, "I was in torture while he was delivering the speech, fearing something would be expected from me in response. I was relieved, however, the people assembled having apparently heard enough."

During the long series of ovations that had followed him everywhere after the close of the war, no one ever heard him say more than a few words in reply to the stirring and long-winded greetings delivered by local dignitaries. Later on when the family was staying at the Dent farm near St. Louis, after a Sunday dinner, while all were out on the lawn on a hot summer's day, little Jesse walked over to a haystack and announced: "I'll show you how Papa makes a speech."

Jesse then climbed up the haystack, looked down at the family and bowed: "Ladies and Gentlemen, I am very glad to see you. I thank you very much. Good night."

By the time the Grants reached London, however, all this was forgotten. Slowly and painfully, but surely, during the years, he had overcome his shyness and developed a gift for putting his thoughts into words. In writing his own orders and dispatches he had always shown a clarity of thought and ability for expression on paper. Self-discipline and practice had enabled him to demonstrate this in verbal delivery. His former military secretary who, as consul at London, had not seen his old chief for six years, was startled to hear Grant at the Lord Mayor's dinner at Guildhall address a brilliant company in language that brought cheers of admiration from some pretty severe critics. As he traveled on in England, throughout Europe, and across every continent, his replies to the speeches of welcome were always fluent, fitting, and often witty or forceful as the occasion demanded.

When news of the success and extraordinary character of the trip started to come back to the United States, the editor of the New York *Herald* assigned John Russel Young, a star reporter, to cover the rest of the trip. Popular demand for first-hand news of the journey increased every week. Within a few months Young's colorful and fascinating dispatches had made the trip almost legendary in the Amercian press. The people looked forward to each new installment. A country which had been primarily concerned with its own growth and expansion and internal troubles now began to face outward and take an interest in the rest of the world, and combined its pride in Grant's acclaim with an avid interest in the places he visited and their people.

As it became clear that his return would be an occasion for renewed popular tribute in the United States, talk of a third-term nomination for Grant in 1880 increased. The former President was reluctant at first. He said, of the letters that he was receiving from politicians, "They have designs on me which I do not contemplate for myself." As time passed, however, his thoughts turned more and more to the possible vindication that a call back to the Presidency would mean. He sincerely felt that his world tour improved his qualifications for a successful new administration. Julia did not conceal her ambition to return to the White House, and there was the thought, too, that he might be able to undo some of the injustices of his successor. Without actively seeking the nomination, he permitted his supporters to begin to gather convention pledges.

The party was divided and there were others whose ambitions stood in the way. The convention began with more votes pledged to Grant than to any other single candidate. For thirty-five ballots his friends held on, but they could not gain the necessary additional votes. The end came when the opposition united on Garfield, a "dark horse" chosen by a stop-Grant coalition, but now Grant had a final opportunity to display his character. One of his opponents, Senator John Sherman of Ohio, recognized toward the end that he could not win, but had enough votes under his control to give Grant a majority. The senator's manager offered General Logan, one of Grant's staunch supporters, a deal: Sherman's votes in exchange for a pledge to appoint Sherman Secretary of the Treasury. When word of this got back to Grant in Galena, where he was sitting out the convention, he wired:

> It was my intention, if nominated and elected, to appoint John Sherman Secretary of the Treasury. Now you may be certain I shall not. Not to be President of the United States would I consent that a bargain should be made.

Grant's political career was over.

39

Memories and Memoirs

★★★★

ONE MISTY NIGHT in November, 1884, Samuel Clemens, better known as Mark Twain, was walking home through the gas-lit streets of New York after having delivered one of his lectures, when two dim figures stepped out of a doorway. They began to walk slightly in front of him, unaware of his presence, and without intending to eavesdrop, he could not help but hear their conversation. His ears pricked up when he heard one of them say, "Do you know General Grant has actually determined to write his memoirs and publish them? He has said so today, in so many words."

Mark Twain, who had just gone into the publishing business with Charles L. Webster, a nephew by marriage, decided when he heard these words, that he had to see Grant at once. The Webster Company intended to publish Twain's own writings and had been formed mainly because of unfortunate experiences he had had with other publishers.

The author of *Tom Sawyer* and *Huckleberry Finn* had met Grant personally several times. He had followed every step in Grant's career and revered him. The writer who had transferred the focus of the nation's imaginative attention to the Mississippi could well appreciate the generalship that had found the key to victory in the Civil War in the opening up of the Great River. He knew that Grant had laughed heartily when he read Twain's *The Innocents Abroad,* while still in the White House, and had been glad to have the writer call on him there.

What made Twain especially eager to see the former President now, after hearing that he was going to write a book of memoirs, was his instant understanding of what a success such a book would be, and how profitable it could be to Grant. Twain knew, as did a shocked nation, how the former President had been financially ruined earlier that year through his own gullibility. The Grants had settled, after the 1880 convention, in a mansion off Fifth Avenue in New York City. They did so because they believed their future to be secure. Ferdinand Ward, who was to prove himself a swindler and a scoundrel, had persuaded Ulysses, Jr., and later his father to join him in a Wall Street partnership under the name of Grant and Ward. The Grants had thought the money was pouring in and trusted Ward completely. For a time the father had associated on equal terms, as he thought, with the New York men of property who had been his friends. Then, literally overnight, the Grants were paupers again. Ulysses Grant had experienced poverty and humiliation before, but this was the worst of all, and friends who had relied on him had lost their investments too.

Stripped of his income, overwhelmed by obligations, disheartened by deception, Grant had to face the world at the age of sixty-two no better off than he had been when he went to Galena at the age of thirty-eight. "I have made it the rule of my life," Grant had said sadly, "to trust a man long after other people gave him up; but I don't see how I can ever trust another human being again."

Twain thought of all this as he entered the Grants' library where he found the General with his eldest son, Fred. "Sit down," said Grant, "and keep quiet until I sign a contract. It's for a book I'm going to write."

Fred had apparently been giving the contract a final reading, and when he was through, his father stepped over to the table and picked up a pen. Twain raised his hand. "Don't sign it," he said. "Let Colonel Fred read it to me first."

When he heard that the contract called for a ten per cent royalty for the author, Twain interrupted and exclaimed, "This is nonsense." He insisted to his startled listeners that the terms were all wrong, unfair, unjust. "That's just an ordinary royalty for an ordinary author," he went on. "You should get at least a twenty per cent royalty, or, better still, seventy-five per cent of the total net profit on the sales of the book."

"No one will pay that," said Grant, "and besides, it's not fair for me to take the book elsewhere. They gave me the idea of writing the book." Twain chuckled at the completely naive attitude of Grant. He insisted that they should not rush into anything and made them agree to wait a day before doing anything. An idea was being born. Fred walked him to the door. "Get him to sign a contract with me," said Mark Twain, "and I'll do the book. I guarantee that if you let me do it he will leave his family well provided for."

"That's just what's on his mind," said Fred. "It's not generally known yet, but father hasn't been well for some time. He has been unable to eat many solid foods, and he's been losing weight. The doctors are afraid that it's cancer of the throat."

Twain was back the next morning, and long discussions followed. Grant consulted George Child, an old Philadelphia newspaper friend, and Child looked over the books of Twain's publishing business. Child firmly explained to Grant that he was under no obligation to anyone just because they had come to him and asked him to do a book—particularly a person as prominent as he, adding, "Different publishers have been after you for years, haven't they?" Grant also demanded to know whether Twain could publish the book without losing money himself on the generous terms he had outlined, and was assured that the prospective demand for the book was such that he could.

Grim and determined, the ailing Grant set to work on the *Personal Memoirs.* He wanted to do an outline of his early years and then to give his own version of the many battles in which he had fought; it was his experiences in the war that the public was anxious to read, and year after year other books of reminiscence or history about the war were being gobbled up.

His whole attitude toward his situation changed. He had been depressed and discouraged after having been overwhelmed by financial troubles again and then beset by the pain of his illness. Death he could not conquer; now he had been given a reason for living that would enable him to conquer despondency. His mind was made up to complete the book for his family's sake, for those to whom he was in debt, and, as he gradually came to feel, for the sake of the book itself.

Some friends came in once, shocked to see him wasting away, and noticed his room covered with maps, papers, and notes. One unthinking visitor said, "The book is killing him." "Not at all," said another, more wisely. "It is keeping him alive. Without it he would already be dead."

"General Grant was a sick man," said Twain later, "but he worked like a well one."

The work on the book began in the library of the house on Sixty-sixth Street near Fifth Avenue. Each evening he would sit and make notes for the next day's work. In the morning a stenographer would come in and he would dictate, clearly, rapidly, and with ease. His son and his old military secretary who were present much of the time, particularly to help in consulting official records, were amazed at his ability to recall and organize the material. He was dealing with battles of two decades before, covering hundreds of miles of territory.

Early in 1885 the newspapers learned that Grant was ill and that he probably would not recover. When the news was out, crowds gathered in front of the house for many hours each day. These were not the crowds of idly curious who congregate when someone is critically ill, for it was not yet at that point. They hardly seemed to have a purpose; many just came to stand quietly a little while, and then moved on. Grant, who had lost sixty pounds, could still walk over to the window and peer out. He suddenly realized what brought them was not the mere popularity to which he was long accustomed. These people could neither see him nor call up to him nor applaud; it was something much deeper—the people were expressing their love for him.

He went on with his work on the book and his race with death. As he continued, the early chapters started to come in from the printers in proof form so that he could look them over and correct them. As he was handling the proofs, he called Fred over. "Doesn't Twain get these?" he whispered. His voice was beginning to go. "Of course he does," said his son. "Then why doesn't he say whether he likes it or not? Shouldn't he say something?"

Twain, who had been immensely pleased with the work as he received it, was startled when Fred came to him and hinted that something ought to be said in the way of encouragement or praise to Grant. "I was as much surprised," he said, "as Columbus's cook would have been to learn that Columbus wanted his opinion as to how Columbus was doing his navigating. It could not have occurred to me that General Grant could have any use for anybody's assistance or encouragement in any work which he might undertake to do."

On the next occasion for him to visit Grant, Twain found an opportunity to turn the conversation diplomatically in the direction needed. He mentioned that he had just been rereading Caesar's classic *Commentaries* on the Gallic Wars and could not help but compare it with the portions of Grant's books that he had thus far received. He told Grant that he saw the same high merits in both books: "clarity of statement, directness, simplicity, unpretentiousness, manifest truthfulness, fairness and justice toward friend and foe alike, soldierly candor and frankness and soldierly avoidance of flowery speech." Grant did not show his reaction except by a twinkle in his eye. He had been too long used to sitting impassively and listening to speeches of praise. He later told Fred that he was extremely pleased.

The work went on. After a while Grant's voice failed him and he could no longer dictate. Weak and wasted away as he was, he insisted on continuing. He demanded a pen: he was only up to the battle of Chattanooga; there were the Virginia campaigns, the siege of Petersburg, the battle for Richmond, the story of Lee's surrender.

In June New York's oppressive summer heat closed in and the struggle became more difficult. Friends offered the use of their vacation home in the Adirondacks, Mount McGregor. As the train, in its journey up the Hudson, passed West Point, he asked to be lifted up so that he could take a last look at its gray buildings, surrounded by towering trees in full leaf and summer shrubbery. He might have thought of how he had hated those buildings when he first arrived, to be greeted as "Uncle Sam Grant."

At Mount McGregor he joined the battle again with his last enemy—a new line was formed on which he was determined to fight it out "if it took all summer." He could no longer walk and spent his last weeks working in a wheelchair on the porch. The passages he wrote there, while wracked with pain, were as even, just, and lucid as all that had gone before.

Toward the end Twain came to visit him. Grant wrote him a note—he could no longer even whisper—asking if there had been enough interest shown in the book for the publisher to be able to assure him that he would not leave his family in poverty. "Advance sales are being made by subscription," Twain answered, "and the money is rolling in. If we do not sell another copy there will be $200,000 for the family." The dying man wrote again, on a scrap of paper, simply: "Thank you." Twain proved to be a good prophet. Four years later he had paid Julia a total of $450,000.

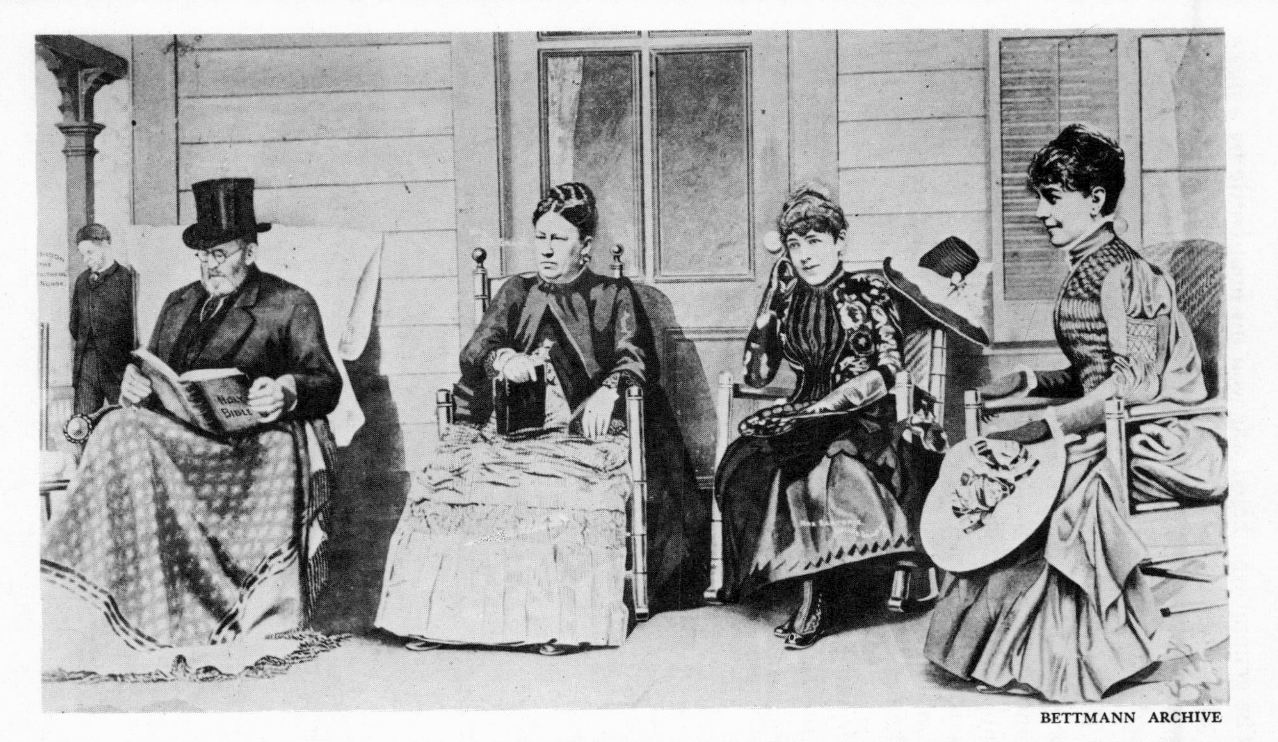

BETTMANN ARCHIVE

Ulysses S. Grant sits on the front porch at Mount McGregor with his wife Julia, his daughter Nellie (Mrs. A. Sartoris), and his daughter-in-law Mrs. C. F. Grant.

The general who hated war won his final battle by a margin of two days. The last page from which he addresses us was written less than forty-eight hours before he quietly passed away:

> I feel that we are on the eve of a new era, when there is to be great harmony between the Federal and Confederate. I cannot stay to be a living witness to the correctness of this prophecy; but I feel within me that it is to be so. The universal kindly feeling expressed for me at a time when it was supposed that each day would be my last, seemed to me the beginning of the answer to "Let Us Have Peace."

He and Julia lie now in a monumental memorial overlooking the Hudson River. Engraved in stone over the entranceway are these words:

LET US HAVE PEACE.

Acknowledgments

One cannot begin to know Ulysses S. Grant without the help of the fine book about his prewar years, *Captain Sam Grant*, by the late Lloyd Lewis. Lewis' letters to his editor, Angus Cameron, published as *Letters from Lloyd Lewis*, constitute a source material of value, and make more poignant the regret that Lewis' death prevented him from completing his projected multi-volume biography. I particularly shared Lewis' pleasure as he reports, his discovery of an 1880 political speech of Grant's:

> He called on the South to drop its proscription of carpet-baggers. He said the West had prospered on carpet-baggers, he said he had been one himself. He said this year was the first time Illinois had not had a carpet-bagger for Governor. It was a shrewd, ironic, penetrating thrust. . . .

Grant's *Personal Memoirs** are not only good source material but also good reading; Young's *Around the World With General Grant* provides almost as much as we get today with the help of a tape recorder: Young in the course of the journey drew out the ex-President on many subjects and incidents. For a century Grant has been the subject of numerous biographers and many of their works have been consulted. Grant's letters have been published in two overlapping volumes by father and son Cramer, and much anecdotal material is to be found in Jesse Grant's *In the Days*

* Collier Books edition, under the title *Grant's Civil War*, edited and with a foreword by Earl Schenck Miers, New York, 1962.

of My Father, General Grant. Ishbel Ross' *The General's Wife* provided useful information on Julia and the children. No doubt further insights and valuable historical data will be found in the complete papers to be published by the Ulysses S. Grant Association.

Many varied sources have been consulted for particular chapters, and it is difficult to record all of one's indebtedness. Forgotten books like Lowell's *Political Essays* help one reconstruct the mood of a period, as does Clemenceau's *American Reconstruction.* Purely military aspects are well handled in British Major-General J.F.C. Fuller's studies and in John Fiske's *The Mississippi Valley in the Civil War.* "The Dawn of Freedom" is based on John Eaton's *Grant, Lincoln and the Freedmen.* The War and the Johnson period have been excellently reexamined in Thomas and Hyman's *Stanton*; Fawn Brodie's neglected *Thaddeus Stevens* is valuable too, and still in print. And above all I must mention DuBois' classic *Black Reconstruction.* The chapter on the gold conspiracy owes much to Henry Adams' essay; the chapter on the 1876 elections exhibits its indebtedness to C. Vann Woodward's *Reunion and Reaction.* The most complete study of Grant's presidency, William Hesseltine's *U.S. Grant, Politician,* is marred by the traditional (until recently) scorn that American scholars have had for advocates of interracial justice. For this reason it must be consulted with care and it is often necessary to check original sources such as Badeau's *Grant in Peace.* The chapter "Memories and Memoirs" is based in part on Mark Twain's version in his *Autobiography.*

I wish to record my indebtedness to, and respect for the memory of, my first editor, the late Oscar Tarcov, who in his tragically shortened life proved himself a friend of man. My wife Sylvette Engel gave generously of her own time that should have been saved for work as an artist and eliminated many faults in style. As usual, errors that remain are my own.